The Problem Art

D

THE PROBLEM ART.

A TREATISE ON
HOW TO COMPOSE AND HOW TO
SOLVE CHESS PROBLEMS,

COMPRISING

DIRECT-MATE, SELF-MATE, HELP-MATE, RETRACTION, AND

CONDITIONAL PROBLEMS.

BY

T. B. ROWLAND AND F. F. ROWLAND.

DUBLIN:
MR. AND MRS. T. B. ROWLAND,
9 VICTORIA TERRACE, CLONTARF.
1887.

LONDON :

PRINTED BY W. W. MORGAN JUN.,
" CHESS PLAYER'S CHRONICLE " OFFICE,
17 MEDINA ROAD, HOLLOWAY, N.

PREFACE.

—:o:—

OUR articles on the Problem Art having appeared in the "Illustrated Science Monthly," "Warder (Dublin Weekly Mail)", and other papers, and many of our numerous friends and readers having requested us to republish them in a complete form, we do so, with additions, feeling sure that our work will meet with that favourable reception which has ever been generously accorded to our writings.

Our chief aim in this little work is to impart to beginners, in as clear and comprehensive a manner as possible, primary instructions on how to compose and how to solve Chess Problems, hoping thereby that they may be induced to cultivate the Problem Art and so sustain one of the most ennobling, intellectual and attractive branches of Chess.

For adepts we have ventured to decide several moot points and have laid down rules for their guidance in the Art of Composing. In doing so we have trodden an unbeaten path, and hope we have not ventured too far.

We sincerely thank all those Chess editors who have so kindly aided by announcing the publication of this work, also, all those who have subscribed. To Mr. W. Geary, of London, we are also indebted for much valuable aid in our writings.

Dublin, January 1887.

INDEX.

—:o:—

THE ART OF SOLVING.

THE ART OF COMPOSING.

PROBLEMS.

DIRECT-MATE TWO-MOVE PROBLEMS.

DIRECT-MATE THREE-MOVE PROBLEMS.

MISCELLANEOUS PROBLEMS.

INDEX.

MISCELLANEOUS.

THE
ART OF SOLVING
CHESS PROBLEMS.

A CHESS PROBLEM is a picture wherein the author can excel just as Raphael, Titian, Turner, Tintoretto, or Paolo Veronese did. The true composer possesses all those rare gifts and special qualities equally with the painter, poet, and sculptor, and it is his genius alone which creates the fancy that holds spellbound the solver. Like the painter or poet, the true composer is born, not made; his brilliant ideas, abounding in beautiful combinations and subtle strategy, in the form of problems, have been aptly termed "the poetry of chess," and as such take a foremost place in chess literature.

The game, ever fascinating, cannot be always enjoyed, as an opponent is not always at hand; not so with problem solving and composing, as a solver can at any time summon up and do battle with a clever though invisible opponent, and thus spend many hours of enjoyment in testing his skill—attacking, repelling, defending and contending—in the same way as if he had a wily antagonist in reality seated at the opposite side of the board.

In order to become a good mathematician it is absolutely necessary that the problems of Euclid be thoroughly understood. Similarly, to become a good chess player we must be able to solve chess problems. Everything played for in the game of chess should be looked upon as a problem to be solved. If it is not "White to play and mate in three moves," it is White to play and win a piece in a certain number of moves. The man who is best able to solve such positions is he who has been in the habit of solving problems. Accustomed to the pretty sacrifices and unexpected moves in which both the beauty and difficulty of a problem consist, he is constantly on the lookout for similar positions when he plays, and if an attempt at a combination is made against him he detects it at the very first move, and is able to turn the operation to his own advantage. It is true there are many strong players who have not studied problems. They have arrived at their position by constant and steady play, which, if discontinued for a short space, would bring them down to a very low level. There is seldom or never anything of a brilliant nature in their play; they will at times overlook altogether a mate four moves deep, which a solver would see at a glance. The reason of all this is, that in chess there are positions which are constantly recurring, and which, if noted and remembered, would teach the line of play to be adopted when any one of them came up. This habit of examining into position is best practised by the solution of problems. If the young chess player who is constantly being defeated over the board tried problem solving for a while he would soon find himself in a position to turn the tables on his opponent.

In examining a problem the solver must bear in mind that he has the author's idea to look for. The key may be well hidden and difficult to find, but once found he is amply rewarded for his labour by the beauties which are revealed. It is similar to raising the curtain from a picture—a work of art—or touching the hidden spring of a musical box which instantly bursts forth into sweet song. The inexperienced solver may have great difficulties to contend with, but we hope that many of them will be overcome by following the instructions we will give in

THE ART OF PROBLEM SOLVING.

THE two essential requisites needed are patience and perseverance; with these many of the deepest compositions may be solved. In saying "patience and perseverance" we do not imply that the solver should prolong a sitting. It is often as injudicious to sit long over a difficult position as to play without reflection; rather lay it aside for some other time than tax your brain too much with it.

There are several ways for solving a problem. The first and best way is to study the position after setting it up on the board; do not move about the pieces, but carefully look into it, and try if possible to detect the author's idea by noting in your mind the result of each of Black's moves. Thus studying, the solver will in many cases, particularly with two-move problems, be able to effect the required mate without finding the key-move, those mates which he cannot effect will then be easily found by altering the position of one of White's men, a little thought and judgment will tell which of White's men will enable him to acomplish the purpose; if successful, the White man moved constitutes the key-move and all is fair sailing. After finding the key in this way, it would be well to write down all the moves which Black can make, reply to each of these moves, and see that in every case the mate is effected. In many problems all the mates may be thus found, excepting perhaps one; when this happens, you have not found the key-move proper, so must commence your work all over again, for it must be remembered that although ten variations out of eleven may be correct, the problem is not solved except a mate is found for each move of Black's. Another method for solving two-move problems is one which has been termed the "mechanical process," a way we would recommend our readers to avoid. Those who adopt it fail to see any of the beauties which always reward the solver for his labour. It is to note down all White's moves, and try each of them in rotation until the solution is found. This is a very sure way for finding a second or third solution if any exists after the author's has been found, and may be utilised for such a purpose.

There are five classes of Problems, viz., Direct-mate, Sui or Self-mate, Help-mate, Retraction and Conditional.

DIRECT-MATE PROBLEMS are those in which White is to play and mate in a certain number of moves, the mate

being effected in the ordinary way, as in an actual game.
Problems of this kind may be divided into two classes:
1st, Attacking problems, *i.e.*, those in which the first
move threatens mate; 2nd, Block positions, *i.e.*, those in
which the key move would not lead to mate were it not
that Black must reply. The latter class may be sub-
divided into two sections—Incomplete Blocks, *i.e.*, those
in which the first move is useful, though such utility only
becomes apparent when Black has moved; Complete
Blocks, or Waiting problems. In these positions the
move is, *per se*, utterly useless, but is the only one that
can be made without interfering with the mates intended
to follow from Black's replies. Of the first of these
classes we give an illustration:

THE ATTACKING PROBLEM.

BLACK.

WHITE.

White to play and mate in 2 moves.

THE ATTACKING PROBLEM is much more difficult to solve
than the "Block position," because the mates are set in the
latter and consequently discernable. To solve the above
position we first look to see if Black could give check.
Finding he could not, we next note the liberty given to
Black's K; he has four flight squares, i.e., squares to
play on. If Black K to Q6, mate follows by Q to Q2,

but we find that we cannot effect mate if he plays KxKt
or any other move. If Black K to B4, mate could be
given by Q to QKt6 if the Kt at Q5 had moved. Likewise, if Black K to K4, Q to KB6 mate if the Kt at Q5
had moved. Now, if the Q's Kt were moved it would
uncover QB's third square and cover Q's fifth, and if
Black's K availed himself of the uncovered square, we
find that Q to Q2 would mate. After a little thought we
come to the conclusion that White's Q's Kt will give the
key, but must consider what move he is to make. Having
the choice of eight moves, we commence to calculate the
effect of each. In so doing we hit on 1 Kt to QB3, and
solve the problem as follows :—

WHITE.	BLACK.	WHITE.
1 Kt to QB3	1 K to B4	2 Q to QKt6 mate.
	1 K to K4	2 Q to KB6 ,,
	1 KxKt or to Q6	2 Q to Q2 ,,
	1 RxKt	2 Q to Q6 ,,
	1 Any other	2 Q to K3 ,,

The first move (Kt to QB3) threatens mate by Q to
K3; Black plays the best moves at his command to
avoid it, hence the variations, of which there are five.

VARIATIONS are the different lines of play White is
forced to adopt after Black plays.

Having studied the illustration given of the Attacking
problem, it will be seen that the idea it contains is the
sacrifice of the Knight in order to limit the moves of the
Rooks, and so allow the Queen to mate, which she does
on five different squares. The sacrifice of a piece on first
move is an idea much in vogue, as many fine variations
follow it. Many instances of self-sacrifice on the battle-
field of real life could be cited. Although the key limits
the moves of the Rooks, it does not restrict those of the
King, which is an important feature in the construction
of problems. The more freedom the key-move gives the
Black King, the better it is.

BLOCK POSITIONS.—Of this class the Incomplete is
thought more of than the Complete Block, as the latter
kind is constructed easily and can be solved without
difficulty.

INCOMPLETE BLOOK.

BLACK.

WHITE.

White to play and mate in 2 moves.

Here it will be seen that White can effect mate after
several of Black's moves. If Black plays 1 K to B3,
White plays Kt at B4 to Kt6, dis. mate; if 1 P moves,
mate follows by Q to Q7; and if 1 Kt at B5 moves, mate
is given by Kt to K7. We find no mate if 1 K to Q5 or
Kt at B7 moves, consequently we look for a move of
White's (the key) which will enable us to accomplish our
purpose and master the position. When Black plays K
to Q5, mate could be given by Q to Q sq, if the Kt at B7
were pinned as the Kt at B5 is. The pinning process
could be done by playing B to Kt sq. Before making
this move we look to see if it would in any way affect the
variations already pointed out: we find it would not. On
the contrary, the B appears altogether useless standing at
R2. All White's men take part in effecting the mates
with the exception of it. The useless position of it would
be an aid to finding the key if nothing else would. Having
played B to Kt sq for White's first move, we watch
the effects of Black's reply of Kt x Q, and find that
mate can be easily given, because, when the Kt at B7
moves, it allows the B to cover Q4 sq, which prevents

his sable majesty from escaping by it. The solution in full is—

WHITE.	BLACK.	WHITE.
1 B to Kt sq	1 K to B3	2 Kt(B4) to Kt6 dis mate.
	1 K to Q5	2 Q to Q sq mate.
	1 P to K4	2 Q to Q7 ,,
	1 Kt(B7) to Q6	2 Q to B3 ,,
	1 KtxQ	2 Kt to K7 ,,
Dual 1 Kt to Q8		{ 2 Kt to K7 ,,
		{ 2 Q to B3 ,,

There are five different mates, consequently five variations. It will be seen that the key-move does not lead to mate were it not that Black must move. In this problem the key-move is useful; it not only pins the Kt when Black plays 1 K to Q5, but covers Q4 sq, when the Kt moves; the utility of it only becomes apparent when Black has moved.

Duals are, as the name indicates, two or more ways of mating in answer to any one of Black's moves. It will be seen in the problem we give that when Black plays 1 Kt at B7 to R6 White has the choice of two different moves in order to give mate, viz., 2 Kt to K7 and Q to B3; this dual occurs three times, that is, once after each of the following moves of Black, 1 Kt at B7 to R6, R8 and Q8. The problem contains only one dual, notwithstanding the fact of it occurring three times, it is merely a repetition of the one dual mate.

COMPLETE BLOCKS, or Waiting Move Problems.—As already stated, in these positions the first move is, *per se,* utterly useless, but is the only one that can be made without interfering with the mates intended to follow from Black's replies. This class is the easiest of all to construct and solve, as the men are merely arranged so that mate can be effected after each of Black's moves. One of White's men is then misplaced without interfering with the mating combination, the replacing of which constitutes the key. Although easy, problems of this class are favourably received, and, when well constructed, have gained prizes in some of our leading problem tourneys. They do not contain any set idea, but in-

numerable, ingenious, and beautiful stratagems are introduced, which are surprising, difficult, and scientific ; this
fact, coupled with their simplicity of construction, render
them attractive to the composer and solver alike.

COMPLETE BLOCK.

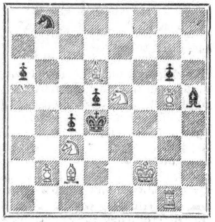

BLACK.

WHITE.

White to play and mate in 2 moves.

The adept's criticism of this problem would probably
be " solved at a glance," for, it will be seen, White can
give mate after each of Black's moves without making
the key, as follows :—

BLACK.	WHITE.		BLACK.	WHITE.
1 B to Kt5	RxB		1 B to Q8	RxB
1 B to B6	KtxB		1 Kt moves	Kt to B6
1 B to K7	KtxB		1 R P moves.	Kt to Kt5

All that remains for the solver to do now is to find
the key; any move on White's part would answer,
provided it would not interfere with the mates. A little
examination will show that all his men are set for the
purpose of accomplishing the mates, with the exception
of the B at B2—that man is the only one that can be
moved without breaking up White's attack. Its purpose
is to cover the squares Q3 and K4, which it could do

equally as well standing at QKtsq, consequently B to QKtsq answers for the key-move, no other could be made, hence the problem is sound. Instead of attacking, White makes a retreating or waiting move which forces Black to play, thus causing him to break up his defence, leave himself open to attack, and allow White to use his forces to advantage, which brings about the final *coup*. Were it not for this waiting move, White would be obliged to relinquish his strong position, and thereby give his antagonist the advantage.

UNSOUND PROBLEMS.—Unsoundness may arise from any of the following causes :—1. When mate can be given to every defence of Black's in less than the stipulated number of moves. 2. When mate cannot be given in the stipulated number of moves. 3. When a problem admits of two or more keys. 4. When a position is impossible or unnatural, *i.e.*, one that could not occur in actual play. An unsound problem is termed "cooked," a term originated by Herr Kling, one of our greatest masters, who, when examining a series of end-games submitted to him by Horwitz, was wont to say, in answer to Horwitz, "Oh, it's a raw idea, is it? well, then, I'll cook your raw idea."

In applying the first form of unsoundness to two-movers, it is simply mate on the move. If the Black P be removed from K3 in the illustration given of the Incomplete Block (page 6), it will be found that 1 Q to Q7 gives mate. Likewise, if the Black B in the Complete Block were at Kt5, White could mate on the move by R x B. Examples of the second form may be found by removing the Black P from Kt3 in the Incomplete Block, then, after 1 B to Kt sq, if Black plays 1 Kt to Kt3, there is no mate. If an additional P was added to either of the Block positions, so that it could move, White would be unable to mate in two moves if that P moved. Problems of the Complete Block order are more prone to the third form of unsoundness than any other ; as an instance, if the B at B2 in the illustration given, were at B5, K4, or Q3, White would have the choice of either B to Kt sq or B to B2 for the key.

IMPOSSIBLE, OR UNNATURAL POSITIONS, are those

B

which could not occur in actual play. Problems are
governed by the laws of the game, and are in reality end-
games; consequently the pieces and pawns employed
should be so arranged on the board that a game could be
played up to the position. Positions may be very improbable, nevertheless they must not be impossible. Naturalness is the due regard to the laws. Two Queens, three
Rooks, three Bishops, &c., of the one colour, though
quite possible to obtain through promotion of Pawns in a
game, are discarded in the setting of Problems. It would
be a difficult task to attempt to describe even one-half of
the impossibilities.that could occur in a problem, so we
confine ourselves to giving a few illustrations only.

PAWN OUT OF PLACE.—When a piece or pawn is out
of place, the problem is unnatural. To describe how
they could be out of place we will take them in their
order, commencing with the P. On referring to the
diagram we give, it will be seen that, in a game, the

BLACK.

WHITE.

White P at QR3 could not be where it is. It is apparent
that it is the QBP, and no legal move or capture could
have got it so placed. On Black's side of the board, the
KRP made one capture, and the QP made two captures;
there being only two White pieces off the board, it

follows that one of these P's is out of place. Now to find out which of them is misplaced, we count the captures made by White. His KBP at QKt6 took four pieces, and supposing that his QBP should be at QKt3, it would have taken one piece; the number of captures would be therefore five, viz., Q, two Kt's, and two R's. To allow the Black KR to play out, the KRP must have made a capture in order to leave a passage, therefore it follows that it is the P at QKt4 which is out of place.

KNIGHT OUT OF PLACE.—Owing to the peculiar oblique move of the Kt, it is seldom charged with making a problem unnatural. Notwithstanding, the position it holds on the diagram is one it could not attain in a possible game. We have shown that all the pieces off the board were captured by P's only. Before the Kt gained KR8 square, the KR played out, and before the KR played out, RP made a capture, consequently the Kt could not have moved from either Kt6 or B7 on account of those squares being occupied; hence the impossibility of the position.

BISHOP OUT OF PLACE.—White's QB is out of place at Q4, and would be out of place on any other square of the board excepting its original square, because of the P's at Q2 and QKt2. It is, of course, possible to capture it on its original square and promote a P to a B; but in this case neither was done, as no piece made a capture, and the eight white P's being on the board show that there was no promotion made. The Black B at QR sq is also in an impossible position on account of the P at QKt2.

ROOK OUT OF PLACE.—The R at KR4 is out of place, and would be out of place on any other square excepting those behind White's KRP and KKtP. The KB not having moved, proves that the KR could not have legally played to where it is.

KING AND QUEEN OUT OF PLACE.—For example, place White's QB on QBsq, and two White P's at QB2 and KB2 respectively, then it will be seen that neither K or Q could have played out.

It is important for a solver to be thoroughly conversant with all the laws of the game, and before taking a

problem in hand to solve, his first care should be to see
that it is natural. In most of our leading solution
tourneys special marks are given for proving a problem
to be unnatural, and in some tourneys no points are
given for the solution of such a position. As a com-
petitor in a problem tourney, the Impossible or Unnatural
position at once receives its death-blow when discovered
to be so. When competing in a solution tourney, having
duly solved the problem, and written down all variations
and duals, a complete analysis of the defences with
pencil and paper is desirable—the "mechanical process."
Take White's men in rotation—K, Q, R's, B's, &c., and
to each of their moves place opposite Black's defences.
This takes time, but the reward comes when a "cook"
is found, and extra points are allotted to you in the
tourney. "Cooks" are frequently unnoticed by the
most expert solver: it is difficult to say why, unless they
are generally captures, or checks, or moves likely to be
overlooked. This analyzing process may also be used to
advantage before sending a problem to a chess editor.
Too much care cannot be taken in examining its soundness ; and if a friend is at hand, it would be wise to ask
for his examination. There is an old adage that "love
is blind," and certainly composers are with regard to
their own cherished compositions.

DIRECT-MATE THREE-MOVERS.—The oft-quoted French
proverb, " C'est le premier pas qui coute " would find an
excellent exemplification of the truth of its teaching in
the solution of a three-move problem, if one might be
permitted to translate, "It is the first move which gives
the solver so much trouble." There must be considerably
more effort required to discover the key move than to
work out the afterplay, for we frequently have the witty
bargain proposed to us, "You tell me the first move and
I'll tell you the other two." It would be wrong, however,
to suppose that the first move is everything in a three-
mover. It must be borne in mind that there remains a
series of two-movers after the key has been divined, and
in some fine problems these two-movers are not at all easy
of solution. We purpose to give the student a few
guiding hints in the arduous though fascinating path into

which he has now penetrated. These instructions, if they are to be of use in most cases, must necessarily be of a general character. Adopting the classification already made in the case of two-movers, our first care on confronting a three-mover should be to inform ourselves of the nature of the composition by deciding (as nearly as we can) to which of the three classes it belongs. "A question well posed is half answered," and the student will find his trouble in this preliminary step well repaid by the satisfaction he is sure to feel in the further efforts he may make to unravel the mystery. He will then first want to know whether the problem whose solution he seeks is an Attacking one, a Block, or an Incomplete Block; and it is to help him in this inquiry that the following hints are offered. The settlement of this question decides the point whether White is to expect any involuntary assistance from Black, or whether he has to do all the work himself, for that is the simple distinction between waiting and attacking. A Block position has been well described as one in which Black is compelled to "hasten his own end." While reading the hints here given the student will do well to keep in remembrance the well-known adage "there is no rule without an exception." Let us first give a glance at Attacking positions. This class in three-movers may be sub-divided into (a) positions where an attack is made on both first and second move; and (b) positions Attacking on the first move and of a waiting character on the second move. The first of these sub-classes is to be regarded as the ATTACKING POSITION PROPER; it comprises not merely the majority of Attacking problems, but the majority of three-movers of all kinds. The second sub-class is hardly deserving of recognition in a classification of three-movers. It is produced by adding to a Block or Incomplete Block two-mover a threatening first move, and is usually overcharged with duals in every variation but the main play. An example of this unwelcome class will be given further on. We will first consider the Attacking position proper. A large number of Black pieces usually demand a threatening first move, and the likelihood of strong measures being required increases in proportion to the liberty enjoyed by Black's forces. The probability approaches certainty when it is observed that the Black pieces preponderate. Black Pawns figure largely in the precautions taken by composers to prevent cooks and dual mates; but it is frequently found necessary to stop their movements. In Attacking problems such checks on their progress are not much needed, and we are there accustomed to see these sable auxiliaries free to advance. This freedom of the Black Pawns is, indeed, one of the surest signs of the Attacking problem. But probably the strongest indication of the desirability of an attacking first move is discovered in the evident freedom to be allowed to the Black King, in conjunction with freedom of action of his Majesty's forces. Such a position generally calls not only for a threat as an initial proceeding, but for checking second moves in addition. These remarks must be understood to be only generally true. A large number of Black pieces are not dangerous when they are each attended by a White piece, and Black's liberty need cause no anxiety when it cannot be used without increasing White's command of the board. A preponderance of Black's pieces over the White ones is not disastrous to the supposition of a Block when it is noticed that the movements of the Black pieces cause mutual obstruction. And with regard to the Black Pawns unchecked in their marching power, it is necessary to discriminate between a position forming part of the problem and one outside the field of operations. One free Black Pawn away from the actual conflict is sufficient to give the Attacking character to the composition. Of course it is not easy to set limits to the action of a problem of whose solution one is ignorant. But we are now engaged in guessing, and this is one of the guesses we must make. Some suggestions with the view of lessening this undoubted difficulty will be made by any by.

The position given on the following page is an illustration of the Attacking problem. It must not be accepted as a specimen of the many fine compositions of the able author, C Planck, M.A., who stands pre-eminent amongst British problem composers, and whose name appears as a prize winner in almost every problem tourney he enters.

ATTACKING PROBLEM.

BY C PLANCK, M.A.

BLACK.

WHITE.

White to play and mate in 3 moves.

Want of space in this small work prevents us pointing out the many reasons for thinking it of this class. The Black Pawns in the middle of the board might, it is true, form part of a waiting arrangement, for we can very well imagine that they might be used to hamper the Black King in his efforts to avoid mate. But the Black Knight is a difficult piece to hold, to say nothing of the advanced King's Pawn. A good rule for the solver to make for himself is, if he fails to see how Black's movements will assist him, to assume the position to be an Attacking one. The key-move is Kt to Kt4, threatening mate on the move by Kt x P. Black has many defences at his command, but the knowledge that forcible measures must be resorted to in every variation will smooth the way of the solver.

THE BLOCK OR INCOMPLETE BLOCK Two-mover extended to a three-mover by means of a threatening first move is to be condemned as an inartistic and unsatisfactory production. We mentioned that such problems were rarely seen. They may be very difficult of solution: this is the case when the two-move portion ·

has the usual appearances of an Attacking problem, as in the accompanying position. The solver will discover to be true here what we stated—that this class of problem abounds in duals outside the main play.

By the Rev. A. Cyril Pearson.

White—K at QR5, Q at KR4, Kt at QKt6, Ps at KB4, K5, QKt2, and QKt5. Total, 7.

Black—K at QB4, Kt at Q4, Ps at K2, K6, Q5, and QR5. Total, 6.

White to play and mate in three moves.

White plays Q to R6, threatening mate by Q to QB6. Black prevents this by Kt to B3, leaving an Incomplete Block two-mover, of which the first move is P to B5.

We will now turn our attention to the second portion of our subject—where White, abandoning the natural course of attacking, throws, as is were, the onus of action on his adversary. The problems to be treated of here have been classified as Blocks and Incomplete Blocks. From the definitions given in treating of two-movers these terms will offer no difficulty to the student. As here used, they apply to the key only; the afterplay of a Block or Incomplete Block being usually attacking. A Block three-mover is seldom continued on the second move, either as a Block or an Incomplete Block; and the same remark applies with almost equal force to an Incomplete Block three-mover. Such "masterly inactivity" as two useless moves in succession is too rare even for a specimen to be readily available for purposes of illustration. It is quite safe to assume in all ordinary positions where variety is possible that the Block or Incomplete Block three-mover is continued by attacking play. The position we now give will serve to illustrate the Block three-mover.

By W. Geary.

White—K at QKt2, Q at K3, B at QB5, Kts at K5, and KKt7, P at QB2. Total, 6.

Black—K at Q4, Kts at QR sq, and K7, Ps at QB2, and QKt5. Total, 5.

White to play and mate in three moves.

Key move—K to R sq.

The characteristics of the waiting problem, whether of the Block or Incomplete Block class, are the converse of those of the Attacking problem. Fewer Black pieces may be expected, the way of Black Pawns barred, the liberty of Black pieces as a rule restricted. It is easy to suggest exceptions to these ordinary signs of a Block. What is stated, however, is true in a general way. The following problem is a very good example of the Incomplete Block ;

FROM AN AMERICAN PAPER.

White—K at QR6, Q at QKt8, R at K2, Kt at QBsq, Ps at KKt2, KKt6, K5, and QR3. Total, 8.

Black—K at Q5, Ps at KKt6, Q4, QB3, 6, 7, QR2, and 4. Total, 8.

White to play and mate in three moves.

This is a more representative position than the others given in illustration of Blocks. The extra Black force on the board to keep off cooks is prevented from moving. Only those pieces whose movements are to assist in the mate being permitted freedom of action. The key is Q to KKt8, and the variations are well worth the trouble of playing over. They will, of course, be all attacking.

The first move of a problem brings into play a piece that was out of play. This statement would appear to be contradicted by many fine problems ; the exceptions, however, are more apparent than real. Experience is the great guide in this as in many other matters. The move that appears the most unlikely to a novice seems the most probable one to the expert solver. The knowledge that there is permitted on the board nothing but what is necessary is in itself a great assistance in solving a problem. We sometimes see a piece so hopelessly removed from participation in the conflict that the mere search for a path between it and hostilities solves the problem. There are cases in which a portion of the force on the board cannot, of its own momentum, come to the scene of action. It is well to remember that if the mountain experiences difficulty in coming to Mahomet there need be nothing to prevent Mahomet from going to the mountain. Frequently the mountain is a White

Pawn three or even four files removed from the Black King (Mahomet). The Pawn can do nothing. We see no reason for supposing it to be a stop-cook. The conclusion is irresistible—Mahomet takes a "constitutional." Zukertort says White Pawns are the mile-stones of a problem—they tell how far the Black King walks. The White King, it may be added, also assists in this duty. The young composer, therefore, will do well to dispense with their use as much as possible if he wishes his compositions to be difficult as well as beautiful. The accompanying position is an excellent specimen of this mile-stone duty, as performed by the White King and Pawns. It is not easy, for all that, the name of its author being a sufficient guarantee for difficulty of solution.

By C. Planck, M.A.

White—K at KKt8, Q at Q3, R at QKt2, B at Q7, Kt at K7, Ps at KR2, QB6, QKt5, and QR7. Total, 9.

Black—K at K4, Kts at Q5, and QR sq, Ps at KB3, KB6, and QKt3. Total, 6.

White to play and mate in three moves.

This is a very fine problem, and it is a further illustration of the Incomplete Block. The key is B to B5.

DIRECT-MATE FOUR AND FIVE MOVERS.—As a three-move problem is a series of two-movers after the key has been divined, so is a four-move problem a series of three-movers. In them likewise we have the Attacking and Waiting moves, and similar sub-divisions. Problems of a greater number of moves are generally confined to a lesser number of variations, and in most cases have only one line of play which forces Black's defence.

On the following page we have a four-mover with a waiting move for key, after which we have a series of three-movers of the Attacking class.

To learn to excel in problem-solving or to gain any benefit from the exercise a hasty, half-careless examination is not sufficient. There must be a careful, logical analysis persevered in until the solution is discovered. Ease and comparative quickness will come with practice, and the practised solver becomes a composer. It is chiefly by solving a composer learns.

BLACK.

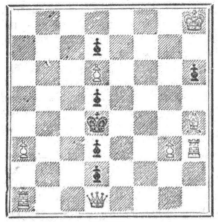

WHITE.

White to play and mate in 4 moves.

The solver would be apt to storm this problem by
such attacking moves as 1 Q to R4 ch or 1 Q x P, but
no other move will solve it excepting 1 B to Q8, which
waits for Black to play. It will be found to contain six
variations, with several sub-variations. The key being a
waiting move is more difficult than one of the Attacking
class.

As an illlustration of a five-mover, in which Black's
moves are forced, we give the following, and as the moves
of problems of a longer range are somewhat similarly
restricted and forced it would be unnecessary for us to
give further illustrations—

White—K at QKt3, Kts at Q3, and KKt5, Ps at K3, Q2,
and QKt5. Total, 6.

Black—K at Q4, Ps at K3, Q3, and QKt5. Total, 4.

White to play and mate in five moves.

White plays 1 K x P, 2 Kt to K sq, 3 P to Q4, forcing
Black to play 3 P x P *en passant*, then 4 Kt (K sq) to B3,
and P mates next move.

Direct-mate problems of from five moves up are not in
general favour now-a-days, as they occupy a great deal
of time to solve, without any compensating result.

SUICIDAL OR SELF-MATE PROBLEMS are those in which White is to play and compel Black to mate White after a stipulated number of moves. The general terms for these problem are " Sui-mates " and " Self-mates," terms which are rather ambiguous, as White does not mate himself, but forces Black to mate him. Black undertakes to *resist* White's design in every move and every possible way, and in no case *assist* in giving the required mate. In this respect Black plays differently to that in an ordinary game; yet all his moves are regulated by the laws of the game, the same as in direct-mate problems. If White desires to be mated in two moves, he plays to attain that object; Black plays to thwart it, and White, after his second move, leaves his opponent no other alternative but to give mate. Likewise, in problems of three, four, and more moves, Black must always make the best moves at his command against White's design.

There is an irresistible attraction about the composing and solving of these problems which is only known to those who give any time and attention to them. They open a wide field for originality, give a larger latitude for ingenuity, and many beautiful ideas and artistic combinations are portrayed in them.

Some years back there was a strong prejudice against self-mate problems, and even still there are a few who are not favourably disposed towards them, and who declare that they are "not chess." The inaccuracy of such an allegation becomes manifest on reflecting that forcing an opponent to give mate is and has been recognized as odds given by an advanced player to a beginner, or weak player. At a chess meeting recently held at Bradford, Dr Zukertort not only gave these odds, but actually specified the P which he would compel his opponent, Mr Mark Dawson, to mate with. The feat was successfully accomplished by the champion. Other leading chess-players have also been in favour of self-mates. Major Jaenisch, the author of several celebrated works on chess, says: "The most ingenious and difficult class of problems of all is that which turns on forcing your adversary to give mate." Howard Staunton was also in favour of them, several self-mates having being published in his popular work, the "Chess Player's Handbook."

Like the direct-mate problems, self-mates may be divided into two classes, the Block and the Attacking. Those constructed on the Block principle we will call Inductive, the others Deductive. In the first the men are so arranged on the board as to give mate to the WK, after which they are removed to different squares, and self-mate in two, three, or four moves, produced at the pleasure of the composer. In the second class an idea is conceived and built upon a basis, and the men so placed as to accomplish the required mate in the required number of moves. According to the former, the men are disposed in a mating combination, and the idea or principle inferred: according to the latter the idea or principle is assumed, and the men arranged and made to conform to it. Of the first we give an illustration—

INDUCTIVE.

BLACK.

WHITE.

White to play and self-mate in 2 moves.

Here we have to replace a piece in such a manner as to give White full control over Black's forces, and form a self-mating combination. We see that neither King can move, and that checks can be freely given on each side. The next thing we do is to note the effects of the checks given to the WK. If B x P dis. ch., WQ must interpose, and we are unable to attain our object. Now if the WQ were off Q's file, and the BQ captured, Black must play B x P, giving mate. In considering what square to play the WQ to, we note that she covers KB3, the other squares around the BK are covered by other men, therefore the WQ must be so placed that KB3 will yet be covered by her, and at the same time be of utility in controlling some of the moves of the BQ. If BQ to QR sq, WQ x Q and mate follows, no further than this can we go in forcing a mate.

We try the WQ on different squares—Kt7 and B6, for instance, then if BQ to QB sq, Q sq, or K sq, she can be captured by a B, and mate is forced. If BQ to R2 or R3, she can be captured by the R, but if BQ x R, we fail to force mate. At this stage we consider, where should the WQ be placed so as to meet this defence? If she were at KKt2 she could play Q x P ch., and the sought-for mate follows. Therefore, for the key-move we try 1 Q to Kt2, and find that it answers. The many variations in the solution are ingenious, and for the purpose of allowing our readers to work it out for themselves, we refrain from giving them. It will be noticed that there is nearly a different variation to each of the Black Queen's moves, she being either captured or forced to give mate.

SELF-MATE PROBLEMS constructed on the attacking principle, which we have termed deductive, are thought more of than those of the Block order. As already stated, they contain set themes which are more pleasing to the solver than the series of forced mates which are to be found in the Block problems. They are of a higher order of construction, and generally more difficult to solve. In them the solver must look for the author's idea or seek for the theme, whereas in the others the solution may be found by a mere mechanical process. It has, no doubt, struck some of our students that the finding of the solution of the problem on p. 21 was a question of time and patience only.

In our next it will be seen neither K can move, and, as the position stands, Black can give mate in several ways.

DEDUCTIVE.

BLACK.

WHITE.

White to play and self-mate in 2 moves.

It will be also found that he has the same power after White's first move. This in no way detracts from the merits of the problem, considering that it is Black's duty to resist giving mate in every possible way. The next thing to be done is to note accurately the position of each of the men, and find out, if possible, the object of having them so placed. The position of the Black Rs show that probably they are intended to give mate by discovery. The Black B appears to be pinned for the purpose of covering Q7. If Black plays Kt x Kt, White could play Q to B2 ch., then mate by discovery follows by K x Q. If Q to B7 ch., White must play K x Q, giving discovered ch., and then the Black K may escape at K7. If the BK were unable to escape, a pretty mate follows by R x R, and so on we keep studying the problem until the author's idea is found. The mate by R x R being so ingeniously arranged, it strikes the solver at once that it is the theme, but the BK thwarts it by escaping at K7. Now if K7 were covered, the mate would be effected. To cover it we try White 1 Kt to B3, and, finding that it answers the purpose, the key-move is found, and the problem is solved.

It will be noticed that after Black plays 1 Kt to K5 or Q6, and White 2 Q to B2 ch., Black has the choice of two moves, viz., Kt x Q and K x Q, either of which gives mate. This choice of moves on Black's part does not constitute a dual. In self-mates, as in direct mates, it is White that has the end to accomplish, Black to resist. If White succeed by two or more different ways, the merits of the problem suffer in degree, but it is no blemish for Black to have several lines of play.

RETRACTION PROBLEMS take the form of end games in which one or more moves are to be retracted prior to playing to effect the required mate. There are two classes, which we will term Legal and Illegal. In the former the position is constructed in strict conformity with the laws of the game, and proof is shown that the moves to be retracted are those which have been actually made. Problems of this class are, as a rule, most ingeniously set, instructive to the solver, and worthy of more attention than what is given to them by the composer. There is some difficulty in their construction which may perhaps be the cause of their not being more frequently composed.

In the latter class the move to be retracted may be any, according to the whim of the composer, which will allow of the mate which follows it. There is no proof to show what the last move was, it is left to the solver to assume that the move to be taken back was the one made. These problems are neither ingenious nor abstruse, and very much inferior to all other classes. They are constructed by simply setting up an ordinary direct mate position and misplacing one of the men, the replacing of which constitutes the retraction. If the conditions of such a problem is "Retract White's last move and then White to play and mate," it simply means White is to make two moves in succession. We dismiss this class as one unworthy of further attention and give our solvers an illustration of the Legal Retraction Problem. (See next page.)

One of the best tests for throughly understanding problems of this class is to play a game up to the position. If the solver succeeds in doing so he will find

LEGAL RETRACTION PROBLEM.

BLACK.

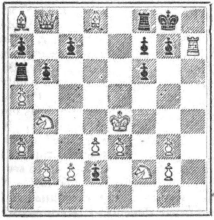

WHITE.

Retract Black's last move, White's last move, and Black's second last move; then White to play and mate in two moves.

---

that he has made the moves which are to be retracted, as such must be made to arrive at the position. A better way is to give the problem an analytical examination, count the number of captures made on either side, and note where each of the men played from, when and how they played, was it by capturing or otherwise. In the above problem we note that White lost a R only, which must have been captured by Black's KP, as its position shows that it made a capture. Black lost six men, the number off the board. His QP at Q7 did not play from B6, as it made no capture, and consequently could not have moved last, neither could his QKtP or KP, otherwise White's Bs could not be where they are. His KRP is off the board—our analysis will presently account for how it was captured. It is obvious that his R at R3 could not have played last, neither could R at KB sq, as then the White K would have been in check, and it is not allowable to suppose that it remained in check. Now the question is, could Black's last move have been K from R sq to Kt sq, moving from a check

D

given by the R? This, we find on a further analysis, could not be, as the White R did not capture Black's KRP, consequently it could not have given check at the square it stands on. None of White's pieces made a capture, the men were taken by his Pawns only, QP at QR5 took three, and KP, KBP and KRP took one each, none of them could have taken a P, consequently it follows that six Black pieces were captured. There are only five Black pieces off the board, also a P, that P is Black's KRP which moved down the file to R8, was promoted to a piece, and duly captured. After all this we find that there is only one possible move Black could have made on his last, and that was Castles, this we accordingly retract. Having retracted it we look to see what move White could have played for his last. All his men appear to be free, that is, not confined as Black's are, and it may appear difficult to determine what his last move was. In this case we look to see what Black's second last move could have been. He did not play K or KR as he was able to Castle after, neither could he have played QR or QP; it is also obvious that he did not play KP x R, in consequence of the B at Q8, but if the B at QR8 were not there, he could have played P to Kt3; consequently, to allow of this second last move of Black's, White must retract a move made with his KB. There is only one square it could have played from, and that is Q5. Therefore B at Q5 to R8 was White's last move, and P at QKt2 to Kt3 was Black's second last move. White for his last move could not have made a capture with any of his Ps, as Kts stand behind QP and KBP, the KP played early in the game to allow KB to play out, and KRP did likewise to allow Black's RP to play to R8.

The conditions of the problem do not ask for more than two of Black's moves to be retracted, yet the solver could demonstrate what his third last move was, viz., R to R3.

One word as to the line of play leading up to the position. It may be considered very bad play, and it would be such were it played as a game, but no matter how improbable the line of play may be, as long as the moves are possible they are sufficient to prove that the position can be arrived at and consequently sound.

Having retracted the moves in the problem we give, White mates by 1 R x R ch, 1 K to Q2, 2 Q x BP mate.

Our next illustration of the Retraction Problem is one founded on B.C.A. Law V., viz. :—"If, in the course of a game, a player move a man when it is not his turn to play, he must retract the said move; and after his adversary has moved, must play the man wrongly moved if it can be played legally."

Knowing this law, the solver will readily find the mate after the retraction. The main point in the problem is to find out the move which has been played out of turn, and which must be retracted.

BLACK.

WHITE.

Black has improperly played two moves in succession. What was the latter of these moves? When found, retract it; and say in how many moves can White effect mate.

This position, originally contributed to "Land and Water," excited much interest amongst expert solvers. To find out what Black's last move was, we must count the number of captures made on both sides, as we did in our last illustration, and account for the position of each of the men on the board.

Black's KP made four captures, all on black diagonals,

so getting to QR6; his QRP made another capture, also on a black diagonal; and as this only leaves the White KB to be accounted for, that piece must have been captured on Black's K3 by the KBP, which Pawn is now standing on K4. White's Pawns made six captures. His KRP took two; his KBP and KP took two between them; and his QKtP took two, thereby reaching QKt8, where it became a Bishop. From the foregoing facts, and what they imply, flow the following deductions :—Black's KBP (now standing on K4) did not stand on K3 on either of the two moves in question ; his KRP, having captured nothing, could not have come to R6 on last move, and for the like reason his KKtP could not have come to Kt4 on last move; his QRP could not have departed from QR2 on last move, and this is really obvious. The Black King could not have moved last, and this is also very clear. Ergo, the Black Pawn now standing on QR6, was played on Black's last move, and it captured something. That something was not a Pawn, seeing that White's QKtP—the only Pawn capable of getting on QR3—is now a proud prelate. Nor could the aforesaid something have been either a Rook or Queen, as in that case Black's King must have been in check during each of the two moves; nor the QB, for that is on the board. It is, therefore, proven that Black, on that second move of his, took a Knight, and hence the solution—1 Kt to Kt5; then Black must, according to the law quoted, play 1 P to Q6, and White mates on next move.

We promised some remarks with a view to setting limits to the possible action of a problem. The subject is beset with difficulties. The exceptions would probably outnumber any rules that could be framed. The value, however, of any rational assistance of the kind could not be over estimated. We offer the following observations to that end. By setting limits to the action of a problem (not the best expression, perhaps) is meant deciding which pieces take an active part in the solution, and in which directions the Black King is to be allowed to move. The movements of the Black King are of most importance, and if they can be guessed with any degree of certainty the discovery of the rest ought not to be far to seek. It is in reply to the question, " What is such and such a piece for?" that we are most likely to get to know which pieces move, and which only do sentinel duty. Having arrived at some degree of satisfaction in the guess at which pieces move, we should try to eliminate the moves unlikely to affect the play, and so narrow the probable operations as much as possible. This should be done with respect to Black's forces as well as to those of White. It would be possible to go into particulars, and give illustrations from problems, but we do not think any good purpose would be served by so doing. The sole intention of these lessons is to induce the student to take up a reasonable, rather then a hap-hazard style of solving, and to really enter into the spirit of the compositions he studies.

If a neat variation is discovered in an attempt to solve a problem the solver should persist in the way he is exploring, as the variation most likely is "in it." If, when the full solution is known, the neat variation is not in it after all, the solver will, if he is also a composer, determine that the neat variation shall not be lost, but shall · form the mainplay of a problem yet to delight the chess public. It sometimes happens than one or two variations are discovered in the required number of moves, while something prevents a complete solution. This generally results from trying a second move as the key. Staunton's advice to the would-be chess player was, " Never lose your temper." Our advice to the Problem Student is, " Never be discouraged."

THE
ART OF COMPOSING
CHESS PROBLEMS.

PROBLEMS are termed the "poetry of chess;" and as "a picture is a poem without words," so is a problem. To the ordinary observer it is merely a few wooden or ivory pieces on a board; to a chess solver it is the hard flint wherein lies the rich amber; the oyster-shell concealing the pearl; the casket that contains the precious jewel; and, as the golden key alone of the owner will disclose the treasures within, so will a gem of problem composition require the study of an adept before the beauty of its inner soul is revealed.

As in a picture the tones should harmonize, and all things tend to throw out the subject in bold relief, so in a problem there should be one idea or theme, and each piece should co-operate in developing the idea to the best possible advantage. In a two-move problem, especially, point and distinctness, with brilliancy and piquancy, are to be the chief aim; and the difficulty of its solution should be in its strategic qualities.

We see hundreds of problems in various tourneys, but how seldom one haunts the memory as "a joy for ever."

To become a good problem composer requires certain qualities and a special taste for the art; for, though any one may learn the method and make a problem, only natural talent can conceive a meritorious theme and compose its setting.

Most people with any taste for poetry can make a jingle of sounds. It is quite possible for a poor player to be a fine problem composer, but it does not follow that a brilliant and strong player can also compose; yet

the qualities essential respectively to player and composer may be found united.

The qualifications necessary for other artistic pursuits
are also requisite in the art of problem construction.
They are ideality or imagination, ingenuity, construc-
tiveness, or invention. Add to these a full measure of
perseverance and patience, and, to crown all, a large
amount of comprehensiveness, in order to grasp the
whole idea, or position, and to know exactly where to
put the finishing touches.

The principle requisites in a chess problem are beauty,
unity, originality and difficulty—beauty of construction
and conception, unity of idea, originality of thought, and
difficulty of solution. The best problems have but one
idea, and only such variations as are required to illustrate
the theme. Poor variations should be cut off at all
hazards. Frequently, in composing, by adding another
"defence," another mate is added, and so on, building up
the problem until it has some ten or twelve variations,
to the detriment of the beauty of the position and the
"unity of idea." Variations, if arising from the original
theme, are to be admired, and it is this very admiration
of them that tempts composers to sacrifice neatness and
unity to the more flowery, and may we say vulgar, style
of overgrown problems. The gardener does not take the
fullest blown rose to the flower show, but the one most
perfectly formed. It is to quality, colour, and rarity
that the judge awards the prize.

ORIGINALITY is a rare quality indeed. With the
thousands of problems that have been composed it is
hardly to be expected that anything new can be further
discovered. Every composer has his own particular
style, and it is in *his* own manner of setting forth some
known idea, or combination of themes, that originality
may be found. The many instances of so-called plagiarism,
where the parties are entirely innocent of copying each
other, show that the same ideas occur to the minds of
different composers.

Artists paint the one scene and sculptors work from
the one model. Take, for instance, the undraped figure
in art; many sculptors have worked on that one subject,

each have rendered their own ideal, and plagiarism could not be brought against them. But if one should perchance copy the folds of drapery, the expression of countenance, or some striking attitude portrayed by another his originality is lost and the charge can be brought against him. Likewise with chess problems, the composer may render some well-known conception in his own way, give it his own dressing, and claim originality.

At the same time when the whole field of thought has been so repeatedly travelled over, that originality in idea is almost impossible, he would be not only censoriously critical but unjust as well, who rigorously investigated the claims of any author to originality of conception. Fancied resemblances and similarity in the elaboration of a train of thought, are quite consistent with the strictest honesty of the composer. Solomon's apothegm that "there is nothing new under the sun," is probably more true relative to the products of mind than of anything else. The thought that flashes like an inspiration across the mental vision of the poet and philosopher of to-day has probably warmed the brain of a Grecian poet or Hindoo sage twenty centuries ago. The witticisms that sparkle and amuse a select coterie in London or Paris, cheered and amused the loungers in the groves of the Academy at Athens before the commencement of our era.

In several instances of similarity of idea which have of late occurred, charges of plagiarism have been brought forward. Such charges are more easily made than proved, and should not exist except in cases where one directly appropriates the work of another, or where one makes alterations in the work of another, and then appropriates it and claims it as his own. H. J. C. Andrews and other reliable authorities give credit to composers for clothing fine ideas in what the problem world would deem presentable apparel. In writing of the Bristol theme, H. J. C. Andrews says, "Many have since extended and embroidered it, and quite legitimately so."

In a Problem Tourney lately inaugurated by the "St. John Globe," one of the conditions were that the problems to be entered should be worked on the theme of giving a White B liberty of action. Many composers worked on this one idea, entered their productions, and the tourney was so far successful that the "Globe" announced its intention of holding a similar one, and invited suggestions as to a theme for illustration. It follows, therefore, that the few censorious critics who are so eager to bring forward mistaken charges of plagiarism could stigmatize every composer who competed in the tourney named.

Literary theft cannot be charged unless a writer appropriates the language of another and claims it as his own. Of such wholesale and thievish transference of mental products it is not probable that much prevails, as the fear of detection will prevent those who are dishonest from copying *verbatim*.

, We do not infer that there is no property in an idea. We contend that a composer is perfectly justified in rendering a known idea in his own particular style in his own original manner. There is property in an idea, and there is likewise property in rendering or redressing an idea known or otherwise.

Similarity of construction is a different thing. There is no property whatever in a position or arrangement of the men. Two problems may be almost alike in appearance and yet contain different ideas. Two or more authors working on different ideas may construct similar positions and each claim his own.

As an illustration we give the following :—

By H Lehner.

White—K at KB2, Q at QB2, B at Q6, P at KKt3. Total, 4.

Black—K at Q5, P at Q4, P at KB6. Total, 3.

White to play and mate in three moves.

By W Geary.

White—K at KB3, Q at QB3, B at Q7, P at KKt4. Total, 4.

Black—K at Q4, P at Q3, P at KB5. Total, 3.

White to play and mate in three moves.

The solution to the former commences with 1 B to B8, and the latter with 1 K to B2.

E

DIFFICULTY is a leading feature, and ranks as high as beauty, unity, originality, and correctness. Most solvers like to be mastered by a problem, so that they may master in turn ; for them there is no spell in an easy problem. One solved at a glance would be worthless and without interest if it were not counter-balanced by some merit, as it would fail in the object for which it was composed—viz., to give pleasure.

"The pleasure of solving a good chess problem is, I think" writes W. W. R., Edinburgh, "usually in direct proportion to its difficulty. Not only is there the satisfaction of mastering the difficulty, but the study necessarily involved makes the solver much more keenly alive to the beauties of the position and strategy by which the mates are effected. Where there is much complexity in the position or variety in the solution, the difficulty is increased, but so is the pleasure. One meets with elegant problems when the solution comes like a flash. The position is admired for a moment and laid aside, and if it is taken up a week afterwards, one has forgotten the solution. However elegant the position, unless it is so masterly as to compel subsequent study, the chances are that in such a case half its beauties are not seen before it is thrown aside like a half-sucked orange. There are other problems whose solution is only reached as the result of careful study. At first sight such a position seems meaningless and chaotic, but as the analysis proceeds it is gradually reduced to order, the force and value of each piece is clearly apprehended, and eventually the composer's ideas are fully grasped and appreciated. The first gleam of light broadens and deepens, and long before the problem is exhausted, doubt gives place to certainty, the solver knows that he is *en rapport* with the composer, and proceeds with deepening interest and increasing enjoyment to exhaust the varieties of the problem and complete his solution. These are the problems which one lingers over with pleasure, and to which one can return without weariness or satiety. If I were asked to give typical examples of such problems, I would refer to Herr Dobrusky's, and that given in the "Field" of the 12th of September 1885. In my opinion difficulty alone is sufficient to awaken interest, although the problem when solved may not secure admiration. I admit that beauty alone is a greater merit, and that a beautiful position with an evident solution is preferable to a problem of greater difficulty but bald conception ; but the fact remains that an elegant composition may be greatly injured by too obvious a solution, and must be improved by subtlety in the stratagem and consequent difficulty in the solution.''

'Tis true that a beautiful position is liable to be impaired by an obvious solution, at the same time, when composing, care should be taken that difficulty does not predominate to the detriment of beauty. Key-moves, in particular, should be well hidden without being separated from the theme. A problem is formed before the key is made, the key is the last touch given to it, and if the key is weak, it detracts from the merits of the problem. It may happen that in order to make a difficult key the position must be altered. It is in thus altering that injury may be done to the beauty of the position ; composers, therefore, must be cautious in considering the effect of a single change, and make provision for a good key when carrying out their conceptions in the main.

The first step for a young composer is to study the known gems of compositions. Take, for instance, a number of prize two-movers ; analyze and endeavour to discover the idea, or theme, that underlies each composition, and the exact duty of each piece and pawn—if this one is to prevent a dual, or a cook ; and mark how the powers of the pieces are utilized, as much as possible, in their position.

To come to the practical part of the subject : there are two methods in the art of composition ; the first is to arrange the men on the board to effect mate, and then to put them back to squares from which they can be played to the original position of mate. The second, and more advanced plan, is to conceive an idea, theme, or combination of themes, and to illustrate it on the board.

The easiest way for a beginner is the union of the above methods, thus : place the men so that Black can be mated in several ways ; then proceed to stop each of

these threatened mates with black men; we then find
that if Black moves any of his pieces, White having to
play can give mate. It now remains to decide which is
the best move for White to put back, so as to form the
key to the problem. Finally, examine each move on
both sides, lest there be a second solution, or a super-
abundance of dual mates. This plan of procedure is to
be recommended for novices to practise, in order to
obtain the complete mastery of the pieces essential to a
composer, as well as to gain an insight into their powers.
Once get this, and beauty will come with study and
practice.

The three great requisites in the construction are
symmetry, naturalness, and economy of force.

SYMMETRY is simply the form of the problem on the
board, and the due balancing of the powers of the pieces.
They should be diffused, and as much freedom given to
their movements as the position will allow. This will
also add to the difficulty of the solution. Though
artistical form is to be admired, yet a clumsy-looking
position frequently evolves itself into diversified and
brilliant variations.

NATURALNESS is the due regard to the laws of the
game, and the possibility of the position. For instance,
suppose all the White forces were on the board, and
Black had doubled Pawns, it would be an "impossible"
position, as none of White's forces have been captured
(see page 10). Three Knights, three Bishops, &c., of one
colour, though quite possible to obtain through promotion
of Pawns in a game, are to be discarded as in bad taste.

ECONOMY OF FORCE is one of the chief beauties in a
problem. Every piece should be of use, and its powers
evoked as far as its position will allow. Superiority of
force on White's side is of no consequence, bearing in
mind this quality of economy of material. Thus Black's
defences may be very subtle, and an apparently over-
whelming force is required to mate. There is a certain
sublety springing from the locality of the squares on
which a problem is composed. Not only may a problem
be solved in a particular position, but often that special
arrangement is far better than another, although both

positions may be equally sound. As a general rule, a problem is more advantageously placed as near the centre as possible; but this admits of frequent exceptions. An unsound problem may sometimes be made sound by shifting it a few squares to the right or left, or by giving the board a half or quarter turn. Nothing looks so clumsy as a double or treble-guard check or cross-check round the King, and he a helpless captive in the centre. The problems giving him one or more squares at the outset are in the best style, or the key-move may free him from a "stalemate" position, and open three or four squares. This is rather a difficult idea, but well 'worth the trouble of composing. The problems wherein the King has some liberty are generally more varied in character, and contain more brilliant variations, than those wherein he stands still to receive his death-blow.

Having mentioned most of the primary features in the construction, we now turn our attention to the

GENERAL RULES.

1. Castling should be avoided except in cases where it can be proved that K and R have not previously moved.

2. Capture of a piece as key-move is objectionable (capture of a Pawn is allowable if intricate, beautiful and numerous variations result from it).

3. P takes P *en passant*, as key-move, is not allowed, except in cases where it can be proved that Black, on his last move, played Pawn two squares.

4. Checking, pinning, Pawn-queening, restrictive moves (moves curtailing the Black King's liberty), as key-moves, are to be avoided.

5. Checking on every move of White is an indication of bad taste, unless there is a great sacrifice of pieces, or unless unusual, intricate, and beautiful mates arise. It may of necessity, however, be allowed in letter, picture, and self-mate problems.

6. The first-moving piece of White should not be placed *en prise* unless there are other pieces attacked, or unless when moved it is placed on a square that is attacked.

7. Never use a piece or Pawn not absolutely necessary

to solve or illustrate the idea. No unnecessary or useless pieces, *i.e.*, such as do not prevent duals or second solutions, or that do not prolong the mate for Black to the required number of moves, should be employed; even in letter and picture problems, it is better to have every piece on duty.

8. Dummy Pawns are not allowed; that is, a Pawn that reaches the eighth square and remains a Pawn. There is much discussion on this point, owing to the "dummy" being theoretically allowed in games by clubs following the B.C.A. code of 1862; but is is better to discard it altogether, as its presence is of doubtful service in problems.

9. Pieces should not be set to do the work of single Pawns; at the same time, a piece may be used in place of a Pawn, under certain circumstances, when a more open position is desirable. If a Knight or Bishop may be used for two Pawns, it is sometimes better to make the substitution.

10. Superiority of force, as regards numerical strength, on White's side is of no consequence, provided economy of material is borne in mind.

11. Two Queens, three Bishops, three Knights, or three Rooks, of one and the same colour on the board, prior to making the key, is an imperfection.

12. Duals should be obviated if possible, without marring the beauty of construction or destroying the main variations. A dual mate, when there is but one variation, is a defect. Duals occurring in the main variations should always be avoided.

13. Avoid crowded positions, and distribute the men over the board with due regard to symmetry and artistical beauty.

14. The best-constructed and highest order of problems are those in which the mate cannot be effected in less than the required number of moves, Black making any defence he may elect, and each of his moves being followed by a different one for White.

15. In general, and briefly, every problem should be so constructed that the key-move is made to appear as the least plausible one.

In view of the foregoing rules, no young composer should become discouraged. The best rule to adopt at the commencement is to construct quite a number of two and three move problems with check on every move. Although they will not admit of publication, they will prepare the way for other, higher, and better compositions, and teach an excellent lesson in the art. No problemist succeeds at first. Of the first fifty problems he composes about twenty-five of them are worthless and never get into print. Always do your best, and at every succeeding attempt you will do better. A distinguished scholar says he owes his success to the faithful observance of this rule—" to believe that whatever could be done by any person, could, if he would take sufficient pains, be done by him."

To compose a Chess Problem, we must first form an idea or theme; without such, the chess-board and men, which are merely the tools used for setting it forth, will not produce any compensating result. The young composer who sits down to construct a problem without first forming a theme is similar to the poet who tries to write verses without having a subject. The poet, painter, sculptor, and problem composer alike must form an idea before resorting to the respective instruments— the pen, brush, chisel, and chessmen—to portray or set it forth. Many young composers spend valuable hours over the board setting and resetting the chessmen in every possible position, with the hope of constructing a problem; but the result is *nil* if the idea is wanting. Such a course acts as a discouragement to their efforts, and deters many from pursuing the art. They commence working in an uncertain groove, like Sir Walter Scott's " Last Minstrel " :

> " Amid the strings his fingers strayed,
> And an uncertain warbling made,
> And oft he shook his hoary head."

It may happen than when engaged toying with the chessmen an idea flashes across the composer's mind, then—

> " When he caught the measure wild,
> The old man raised his face and smiled ;
> And lightened up his faded eye
> With all a poet's ecstasy."

IDEAS may be formed by observation—trying experiments with the pieces, solving the problems of others, playing actual games, or watching others playing. They may also be formed without observation—some pretty mate, or series of mates, ingenious sacrifice, subtle *coup*, or deep stratagem, may enter the composer's mind without being sought for. Again, a composer may think out a theme, or select a piece or Pawn, and arrange a position so as to enable it to effect as many different mates as it has power to give, moving from one particular square. Effecting mate by discovery is a theme much in vogue of late.

A White K, standing before a Q, R, or B, can give discovered mate by moving to one of six different squares. The squares may be covered or guarded by Black's men; but a position can be so arranged that when Black is to play, he is forced to remove one of his guards, and so allow WK to play. The following is an illustration:—

White—K at QB6, Q at QKt sq, Rs at KB3, and KR4, B at KR8, Ps at QR2, K3, and KKt2. Total, 8.

Black—K at K5, Bs at KB sq, and KKt5, Kts at QR sq, and KKt6, Ps at QR3, 5, and 6, Q6, KR3, and 4. Total, 11.

White to play and mate in two moves.

Key: 1 Q to Kt7.

A Queen can effect as many as twelve different mates, moving from one square. The following is a good specimen of this class; it contains sixteen mates, twelve of which are given by the Q:—

By J. PAUL TAYLOR, F.R.H.S.

White—K at Q8, Q at Q3, Rs at QKt7, and QB7, B at KR4, Kts at K7, and KB7, P at QB2. Total, 8.

Black—K at K3, Q at QR7, Rs at QKt3, and K8, Bs at QB sq, and KB sq, Ps at QR2, and 6, QKt5, KKt2, 3, and 6, and KR2. Total, 13.

White to play and mate in two moves.

Key: 1 K to K8.

A Rook standing before a B can give dis. mate by moving to one of fourteen squares. For instance, place

Black K at KR sq, WK at Q8, WB at QR sq, and WR at QKt2. To give dis. mate by moving R to one of the fourteen squares which it commands, we must cover KR7th and KKt8th squares. This may be done by placing a WB at KR7 and a WR at KR2. Now, in order to make a problem, we must prevent the R at Kt2 from moving to more than one square at a time. Place a Black R at KR8, and, to prevent it from capturing the B, a WKt at QKt sq. Now, if Black plays 1 R x R, White must play R x R giving dis. mate. If Black R to K, Q, B, or Kt 8, White R at Kt2 must move to prevent Black R from interposing. Again, if Black R x Kt, White R x R dis. mate. Now place a WKt at QKt8, WP at QR2, and a Black R at QR sq, the effect will be found the same as in the case of the Black R at KR8.

Our position is as follows :—

BLACK.

WHITE.

All that remains to be done now is to make a key-move. Our General Rules give those key-moves which are to be avoided. The key-move to be adopted should be one that will hide the idea, be difficult to find, and be without any of the objectionable features named. A problem mainly depends on the difficulty of its key-move, in the same way as the construction of an arch depends on the

F

soundness of its key-stone. The construction may be perfect in both cases, but if the key-move is obvious, or the key-stone weak, the fabric is liable to fall to the ground.

In the problem before us it is hard to hide the idea, as the R at Kt2 cannot be misplaced. Kt from B3 to Kt sq would do; it becomes sacrificed to save the B—a feature which will in some measure atone for cutting off one of the squares from Black's KR. It will be noticed that were it not for the check by QR x Kt, White could give dis. mate by playing R to any square of the file on which it stands.

A Bishop standing before a R can give dis. mate by moving to one of thirteen squares. To illustrate the Bishop's power, place WB at Q5, WR at KR5, and BK at his QR4. To effect the mate intended to be given, we must cover the squares round BK. This may be done by placing WK at QR3, WB at QR7, and WKt at QKt8. Now, as in our previous problem, we must prevent White from having the choice of more than one square to play to. We accordingly enlist the service of a Black R and place it at Black's Q8 sq. Now, if Black plays R to any square of the rank, he prevents White from having a choice of moves; but if Black plays R to a square on Queen's file, White cannot mate, therefore place a Black P at Q7. A like result will be arrived at on the other side of the board by placing a Black R at Q sq, Black P at Q2, WP at Q6, and WKt at KKt8. The object of placing WKt's at QKt8 and KKt8, is to prevent Black R to QR sq and KR sq, because if R to QR sq, White would not be confined to one move only, and if R to KR sq, no mate could be given, as Black could then capture WR. We now examine to see if there are any duals, and find that if Black K to Kt4, White would have the choice of four moves, consequently we place a WP at QR4 to prevent K to Kt4. Our next step is to make a key; the piece to misplace is of course the R, as it is the most likely piece to hide the idea. Any square on the file would do to place it on except R sq and R8. The former is objectionable, as the key would be moving a piece out of *en prise*; the latter is objectionable, as standing at it the R would appear to be out of action, and it would be obvious that it should move. In misplacing a man, care should be taken to select a square from which it would appear to have some motive in standing on. We place R at R3. At that square it may appear as if it had some bearing on QKt's file. Finding that the position admits of no other solution, our task is accomplished and the problem completed.

The position is as follows :—

White—K at QR3, R at KR3, Bs at QR7, and Q5, Kts at QKt8, and KKt8, Ps at QR4, and Q6. Total, 8.

Black—K at QR4, Rs at Q sq, and Q8, Ps at Q2, and Q7. Total, 5.

White to play and mate in two moves.

A Knight standing before a R can give dis. mate by moving to one of eight squares. As an illustration we give the following, the key of which is 1 Kt x P.

White—K at QKt8, Q at QKt6, Rs at QR3, and KKt4, B at Q sq, Kts at QKt4, and Q5, Ps at Q2, and KB6. Total, 9.

Black—K at QB5, Q at KB8, B at K sq, Kt at KR sq, Ps at QKt4, QB4, KB2, 5, 7, KKt4, and KR3. Total, 11.

White to play and mate in two moves.

This circular tour of the Kt is an idea which can be carried out in a three-move problem equally as well. For illustration see " Chess Fruits," page 74.

It will be seen that the power and range of each piece can be fully exemplified in problems. Seldom does a position occur in a game in which the full power of a piece is utilized or shown to advantage. This fact alone would stamp problems as the soul of chess, and enable them for ever to unfold instruction even to the most advanced player.

Even the humble Pawn, when standing on its original square (RP excepted), and supported by a Q or R, is invested with the power of mating in six different ways. Standing at K2, with a Q at K sq, and Black K at his

5th, the Pawn could mate by advancing if K played to B4, B5, Q4, or Q5. It could also mate by making a capture on either side. This theme we will lay aside for the present, as it cannot be worked out in a two-move problem. It has been carried out in a three-mover. See "Chess Fruits," page 139.

In order to construct a two-mover in which the KP is to mate, our idea will be to give Black K two squares to play on, and mate him on each. Place Black K at K6, Black P at K5, WP at K2, and WQ at K sq. Black can now play K to B5 or Q5; when he plays our object is to advance P, giving mate. Play K to B5, followed by P to K3. This is one of the mating positions; now cover the squares round the K. In covering the squares men should be used, if possible, which will be of further use in the position. WK must be on the board, and, like any other piece, be of use, consequently as it could cover two squares or three, place it at KR5. To cover B3 and B5, place a WKt at Q4; standing thus it will be found otherwise useful later on: Black P at K4 effectually covers the last square, and Black, having no escape, is check-mated. Now retract the moves, and play KxKt, again followed by P to K3. Here again we must cover the flight squares, WKt at KB4, WPs at QKt3 and QKt4 answers the purpose. Retract the moves again, and we find that Black has choice of four moves, two of which admit of mate, and two as yet untried—they are P x Kt at B4, and P x Kt at Q4. If the former, Kt at Q4 mates, and if the latter, Kt at B4 mates. On examining further, we find that each Kt gives a dual mate. This defect may be remedied by placing a Black P at K3. Finding no other mate, we make a key. In this case the Q is the piece to misplace. Misplacing any other man will not do, as standing at K sq the Q would at once betray the solution, and the solver would lose any pleasure which seeking for it would afford. Having six squares to choose from, we select KR4. Standing at that square, it would appear as if Q was guarding the Kt at B4. The key, Q to K sq, cuts off one retreat and gives another, which is allowable; moreover, the sacrifice of the Kt is a good feature.

Position—

BLACK.

WHITE.

White to play and mate in 2 moves.

The following ingenious problem by H. W. Sherrard fully illustrates the power of a WP when standing on the seventh rank.

White—K at QR2, R at KR7, B at Q6, Kts at QB3, and K3, Ps at QB6, and KR4. Total, 7.

Black—K at K3, B at K sq, Ps at QB4, QB5, and Q2. Total, 5.

White to play and mate in three moves.

It will be seen that after the key move (1 P x P) the P must be promoted to a Q, R, B, or Kt, according as Black plays.

Having shown how ideas are formed which illustrate the full power of a White piece, we will turn our attention to ideas which illustrate the full power of a Black piece.

Liberty to the Black K is an important feature in problems, and one which all young composers should give attention to. In many cases judges of tourney problems allow a certain number of marks for freedom of BK, as they consider such freedom to be an essential point.

The greatest number of flight squares that can be

given to a Black K in a two-move problem is seven. It can be given the maximum amount in three-movers. Two-movers in which seven squares are given are rare, as they are difficult to construct, and owing to the amount of liberty given, the solutions commence with a check.

In a Problem Tourney recently inaugurated in a West Indian paper, two small prizes were offered for the best and second best flight square problems. One competing position gave BK seven flight squares, another gave five. Although of the *Solus Rex* class each was meritorious, and under such circumstances it was reasonably supposed that the seven flight square problem would have gained first prize. Such an event, however, did not happen, as in this case the judges disregarded the plan of allowing marks for flight squares and awarded first prize to the five flight square problem. They may have considered the ch on first move a blemish, but it could not be considered so until it can be shown that the idea can be carried out without it.

The problem referred to is as follows:

By W. Jay N. Brown.

White—K at KKt8, Q at QKt8, Rs at KKt2, and K8, Bs at KR sq, and KB8, Kts at KR3, and QB2, Ps at KKt4, K2, K7, and QR4. Total, 12.

Black—K at Q4, Rs at Q sq, and Q6, Ps at QB2, and Q2. Total, 5.

White to play and mate in two moves.

The following is another illustration of the same kind :—

By F. C. Collins.

White—K at QR7, Rs at QB sq, and KR7, B at QB3, Ps at Q5, K4, and KKt7. Total, 7.

Black—K at Q2, R at K3, Kt at Q7, Ps at QKt4, and Q3. Total, 5.

White to play and mate in two moves.

As another illustration we give the following. In it, it will be noticed, the Black K is not forced to move—

By W. B. Huggitt.

White—K at QR2, Q at QKt8, Rs at Q2, and KR4, B

at K sq, Kt at KB6, Ps at QKt3, QKt7, and K2. Total, 9.

Black—K at QKt4, Q at Q5, Kts at QR sq, and QR5, Ps at QR6, and QB4. Total, 6.

White to play and mate in two moves.

These are the only seven flight-square two-movers that have come under our notice. The solution to the first commences with 1 P to K4 ch; the second, 1 P x R ch; and the third, 1 P x Kt ch.

As an illustration of a three-mover giving the maximum amount of liberty we give the following :—

White—K at Q sq, Q at QR7, R at Q8, Bs at K7, and KR3, Kt at KR5, Ps at QB5, QR2, and QR3. Total, 9.

Black—K at Q5, Ps at KKt5, Q3, and QR5. Total, 4.

White to play and mate in three moves.

Solution—1 Q to Kt8, 1 P to Q4 (a), 2 K to Q2, 2 any, 3 Q mates acc. (a) 1 K to B file (b), 2 R x P, 2 any, 3 Q to Kt4. (b) 1 other, 2 Q x P, 2 any, 3 mates acc.

Six-flight two-movers are numerous, as they are less difficult to compose. They are of the waiting move class, and in most cases mate is effected by discovery. As an example, place BK at K4, WR at KKt3, WB at KR2, and WKt at K7. Here Black may play to one of six squares; when he does so our object is to give mate. Play K to B3 followed by R to Kt6. To make this one of the mating positions we must protect the Kt from capture and cover KB7 square. WK at K8 answers both purposes and Black is mated. A similar mate occurs if K to K3, but if K to Q3 there is an escape at B4. This can be stopped by placing a WP at QKt4. Now replace R at Kt3 and K at K4, and try the effects of K to B5. Here we must build up another mating position. A White B at K2 would cover KB3, KKt4, allow R to mate at Kt4, and be of further use. Consequently place WB at K2, and move R to Kt4 to give mate. K could escape at K6; this we prevent by placing a BP at K6. Black is mated in a similar way if K to K5, but if K to Q5 we find that he has another loophole at QB6 which may be stopped by placing a WP at QKt2. Replace K and R again, make a suitable key, and our task is accomplished. B from Kt sq to R2 would do as key move.

The position is.as follows :—

White—K at K8, R at KKt3, Bs at K2, and KKtsq, Kt at K7, Ps at QKt2, and 4. Total, 7.

Black—K at K4, P at K6. Total, 2.

White to play and mate in two moves.

This is a very simple position, as it is of the *Solus Rex* kind, but it needs no excuse, as many of the finest positions were simple in the first stage of their construction. To improve it Black should have some other free men on the board, so that his K need not be forced to move, but in adding a Black man several other White men may be required. Adding White men thus would not detract from the merit of the problem—(Rule 10). " Superiority of force, as regards numerical strength, on White's side is of no consequence, provided economy of material is borne in mind." The position could be improved by placing a Black B at Black's QKt3, and WR at QR6. These additions save his sable majesty from being forced to move, and do not interfere with the mates. If B moves, White plays R to Kt4, giving dis. mate.

The greatest number of squares a Q can command is twenty-seven. It is possible to compose a good problem giving that number, but difficult to do so without dual mates. Several problems giving the full liberty have been published, but we have not seen one free from the *bête noire*. To avoid the duals the liberty would have to be curtailed, and as curtailing the liberty would be thwarting the author's idea, the duals were allowed to remain.

A prize was offered in a Problem Tourney, inagurated by the " Sheffield Independent," for the best position giving Black Q most liberty. Four were entered, giving 27, 21, 19, and 7 squares respectively. The judge (Mr. F. C. Collins) awarded the prize, not to the 27 square problem, but to the 7 square one, because he considered it to be the best. It contained no duals, whereas the others did. This shows that it would be better to confine the liberty than to admit duals.

To command 27 squares place Black Q on one of the centre squares of the board. For illustration we select Black's K4. Next place BK at QR sq, WB at QKt8, and WR at KR8. Our design is to give dis. mate by B x Q. To carry it out we must prevent K from escaping at R2 and Kt2, but before stopping these squares we must try some of the Q's moves, so as to be able to select covering or guarding pieces which will be of further use. If 1 Q to any square on the diagonal which B commands, B x Q. If 1 Q x B, we see that we must arrange to mate in another way; therefore we try a WR at QKt sq, and BP at QR2. Now, if Q x B either R x Q mate. On replacing Q and B we try 1 Q to K5, 6, 7, or 8, and find that dis. mate can be given by B to K5; but if 1 Q to K sq K2, K3, or P moves we cannot mate. In this case stop the advance of P by placing WKt at QR6, then if 1 Q to K sq, or K3, Kt mates at B7. The same mate can be given if 1 Q to K2 by placing a BP at Q2, so as to protect the Kt. Kt can also mate if 1 Q to KR4, KKt4, KB4, and Q4; but no mate occurs if 1 Q to QB4 or QKt4. By playing to the latter square the Q cuts off the range of the R at Kt sq; we must therefore place a WP at QB6 to recover Kt7 sq, also to enable Kt to mate at B7, when Q plays to QB4. If 1 Q to QR4, B to B7 dis. mate. If 1 Q x KR or plays to any square of the diagonal running from right down to left, Kt mates. Our next step is to place WK on the board. Owing to the great sway of Black's Q it would appear difficult to find a place of safety for the K, as it may be checked on any square. A check given from the diagonal which B commands would be of no consequence, as B can take Q; consequently we will place WK at KR3. To prevent other checks place Black Ps at KR5 and KB6, and WP at KKt4.

So far we have succeeded in giving Black's Q the maximum amount of liberty, but like the competing problems which were debarred from winning a prize, it contains duals.

The initial position is as follows :—

White—K at KR3, Rs at KR8, and QKt sq, B at QKt8, Kt at QR6, Ps at QB6, and KKt4. Total, 7.

G

Black—K at QR sq, Q at K4, Ps at KR5, KB6, Q2, and QR2. Total, 6.

It contains 8 variations and 4 dual mates. The variations are caused by Q playing to each of the squares the B commands, B x Q on each; if 1 Q x B, R x Q; if 1 Q other, Kt mates. Kt also mates if 1 P to Q3, and B mates if P to B4 or P x P. The duals are—If 1 Q x B either R mates, if 1 Q to B2 either Kt or B x Q mate, if 1 Q to QB4, B to Q6, or Kt to B7 mate, and if 1 Q to K5, 6, 7, 8, Q5, QB6, or QR8, Kt to B7 or B to K5 mate. The latter dual is the worst as it is so often repeated. It could be avoided by placing BPs at K5 and Q5, but as our idea is to give the Q full liberty we refrain from so placing them. Our next step is to adopt a key. This we find to be a difficult task to accomplish, owing to the strong attack of White. As the position stands White threatens mate by B x Q. It would be useless to misplace the R at R8, because if it were at say KR6 White could mate in two moves by 1 B x Q and 2 R to Kt8. It follows that to make a suitable key the position must be revised. It can be revised in many ways. One way is to exchange the Black Ps at Q2 and KB6 for WPs. Then, with KR standing at KR6, White could not effect mate in two moves by 1 B·x Q, for then Black, not having a move to make, becomes stalemated, and White's design is defeated. Another and better way is to remove the WR at Ktsq and place a WKt at KB8. Then for key play Kt x P. According to rule 3, capture of a P as key-move is allowable under certain conditions. In this case it is preferable, as it enables us to economise force and give Black more freedom of action, and avoid one of the dual mates. We give the final position on the opposite page.

When the composer has mastered the movement of the Black Q he can readily work out ideas giving freedom to a Black R or B. The difficulty of doing so is 50 per cent less, as the Q combines the power of each. With either R or B the subtle *coup de repos* may be more easily formed, variations more numerous and elegant, and the problem rendered more piquant and pleasing.

Problems giving freedom to a Black R have engaged

Final position giving Black Queen full liberty, referred to on opposite page—

BLACK.

WHITE.

White to play and mate in 2 moves.

---

the attention of many composers of late, and have gained high honours in problem tourneys. The first prize winner in the Irish section of the "Irish Sportsman" Tourney, which we give, allows Black R the maximum amount of liberty, and contains 11 variations, 7 of which are caused by moves of the R.

By Mrs. T. B. Rowland.

White—K at KR7, Rs at K7, and KKt3, B at QKt sq, Kts at KR5, and KB3, Ps at KR4, K2, and Q3. Total, 9.

Black—K at KB4, R at QKt5, B at KR3, Kt at Q sq, Ps at K6, and Q3. Total, 6.

White to play and mate in two moves.

Key : 1 R to Kt6.

The second-best problem in the English section of the same tourney contains 11 variations. The Black R has 7 moves and causes a variation on each.

The position is as follows :—

By J. G. Chancellor, M.A.

White—K at KKt5, Q at KB sq, Rs at KR5, and KKt6, Bs at K2, and QKt6, Kts at KB3, and QB6, Ps at Q3, QB5, and QR3. Total, 11.

Black—K at Q4, R at Q5, B at KB sq, Ps at QKt2, and QR5. Total, 5.

White to play and mate in two moves.

Key: 1 Q to QKt sq.

The first prize winner in the recent Tourney of the " Sheffield Independent," which is as follows, allows Black R nine squares to play on, and contains eight variations, six of which are caused by the R's movement.

By T. Taverner.

White—K at Q8, Q at KR2, Rs at QB3, and K3, B at KR3, Kts at Q6, and K7, Ps at KKt4, and QKt5. Total, 9.

Black—K at Q5, Rs at KR4, and Q8, B at KR3, Ps at KB5, and Q7. Total, 6.

White to play and mate in two moves.

Key: 1 B to B sq.

The following is another illustration of the same theme. It contains ten variations, seven of which are caused by the R.

White—K at QKt7, Q at KKt2, R at QB7, B at KKt sq, Kts at QKt5, and QR6, Ps at KB3, 6, Q2, and QKt4. Total, 10.

Black—K at Q4, R at KB5, Kt at Q2, P at K3. Total, 4.

White to play and mate in two moves.

Key: 1 B to R2.

Many fine problems may also be constructed by introducing the second Black R and giving it liberty also. As an illustration of this kind we give the following—

White—K at KR sq, Q at KR2, Rs at KR5, and QB2,
Bs at K2, and Q6, Kts at Q8, and QR sq, Ps at KB3,
and K6. Total, 10.

Black—K at Q5, Rs at QB5, and K5, B at QR7, Ps at
K6, QB2, and QKt4. Total, 7.

White to play and mate in two moves.

Key: 1 B to Kt4.

Each of the positions we give will repay a careful
study, as they fully illustrate the power of a Black R,
and show the numerous variations it causes and the
many ingenious and pretty mating positions it forms.

There is little or no difficulty in placing a Black piece
on the board and constructing a problem which would
allow it full liberty of action. The art lies, not in giving
a piece liberty, but in giving it command over the
opposing forces, and so cause White to vary his play.

A Black B may be placed on the centre of the board,
and a problem constructed on the same lines as the one
we constructed giving Black Q liberty, but such a problem would be deficient in point and piquancy as there
would be only one or two variations of any note. We
have seen many problems wherein a Black B causes four
and five good variations. The competing problem in the
I. C. A. Problem Tourney bearing the motto "No, Sir"
is a good specimen of this class; of the nine variations
it contains, the B causes four. Our position illustrating
the moves of the WK is also another good specimen.
The latter may be said to contain two ideas, one is giving
discovered ch by moving WK, the other is giving the
Black B liberty.

Now we will compose a problem with the idea of
giving Black B liberty, and making each of its moves
vary White's play. Place Black B at QKt sq, from that
sq it commands the diagonal running down to the right.
To effect a different mate after each move we must consider what pieces to employ, and where to place BK.
Place BK at K5 and WKt at KB5; now, if B plays to
Q3 or Kt6 WKt could take B and give mate in each case
provided the squares around the K were covered. To
cover them we must select pieces which will be of further

use. Place WRs at QB5 and KB2, by so placing them
we protect the Kt, cover 4 squares, and can arrange
mates, when B plays to K4 or KB5, by R x B in each
case. To enable either. R to take B without being
captured in return, place a WKt at KKt6, and to enable
Kt to give mate by taking B, place WPs at QB3 and Q2.
The only escape now is at Q3 sq, which may be stopped
with a BP. In order to give mate when B plays to B2
or R7 place a Black Q at KR2, and WQ at QKt sq;
then if 1 B to B2, 2 Q to Kt7 mate; and if 1 B to R7, 2
Q to KR sq mate. If B plays to R2 there would be a
series of duals; consequently prevent it from doing so
by placing a BP at QR2, and to prevent the P from
moving place WK at QR6. The next thing to consider
is the moves of BQ. It will be noticed that if she moves
White can give mate at either KR sq or QKt7, but if 1
Q x Kt there is no mate, as then BQ could cover; a WP
placed at KB6 would prevent her from interposing on
the Q's side, and mate is effected in all cases.

In examining further we find that W can give mate on
the move at either K sq or Kt4. This may be prevented
by placing a BKt at Q6 instead of the BP. There is
one dual mate if Black plays 1 Q to R8, by 2 Q x Q or Q

BLACK.

WHITE.
White to play and mate in 2 moves.

to Kt7. A similar dual would occur if 1 Q to QKt2 were it not for the ch. A key move may be made by playing Q from B2 to Kt sq.

Our next idea is to give liberty to a Black Kt and make each of its eight moves cause a different variation. Owing to its peculiar move many fine problems can be constructed with this theme and each be rendered differently. One way is to place the Kt before a masked battery, so that when it moves the battery can open fire with a double check and mate, or else capture the Kt with one piece, so as to prevent it from interposing, and give discovered mate from another. Another way is to place a guard on each of the squares the Kt can play to, so that it may be captured and mate effected when it moves.

We will construct a problem on each of these principles, and so demonstrate how the one idea can be differently rendered. As in our previously constructed problems, we will work on the crude idea only, leaving it to our readers to elaborate and give it the artistic finish.

Taking the idea with masked battery first we proceed by placing Black Kt at K4, from which it commands eight squares. If it plays to Q2, KB2, KKt3, or KKt5 it could be captured by a R standing at KKt7. Therefore place WR at KKt7; form the battery by placing a WQ at KR8, and, in order to give dis. mate, place BK at QB6, and cover the squares around it. WK placed at QR4, WB at QBsq, and BP at QB7, covers five of the squares. To effect mate when Kt plays to either B5 or Q6 we must select covering pieces for those squares which will aid us. B4 may be covered by placing a WKt at QR3; then if Black plays Kt to B6, the WKt is at liberty to give mate. Another WKt placed at KB4 would cover Q3 sq and give mate in a similar way if Black plays Kt to Q6. As the position stands a dual mate occurs after each move of the BKt by R to Kt3 or QB7. This can be prevented by placing WPs at KB3 and QB6. Then If 1 Kt x KBP, 2 R to Kt6, pinning the Kt and so preventing it from interposing. If 1 Kt x QBP, 2 R to QB7 giving dis. mate in like manner. So far we can give mate after each move of the Kt, but it

will be seen that the Kt is not forced to move, as Black
can play 1 K to Q5. As far as the moves of the Kt are
concerned, it is not necessary to guard Q5 sq, as the Q
covers it in giving mate; therefore we will leave the
square open and arrange a mating position to provide
against further escape. Place White Pawns at QKt4
and KB2. Now if 1 K to Q5, 2 B to Kt2 mate.
A good key would be Q from QR8, or KR sq to KR8;
but at either of these squares the Q would cause a second
solution by giving check, forcing the K to move and
allowing B to mate. It follows that it would not do to
misplace the Q, neither would it do to misplace the R,
as then White could mate on the move by 1 Q x Kt. We
must therefore misplace a Kt. Remove the Kt at B4 to
K6 for key. We finally examine our position, and finding it sound, our masked battery idea is portrayed and
the problem completed.

The position is as follows :—

White—K at QR4, Q at KR8, R at KKt7, B at QB sq,
Kts at QR3, and K6, Ps at QKt4, QB6, KB2, and KB3.
Total, 10.

Black—K at QB6, Kt at K4, P at QB7. Total, 3.

White to play and mate in two moves.

Our next illustration of the Black Kt's circular tour
will show how a guard may be placed on each of the
eight squares the Kt can play to so as to capture the Kt
after it moves and give mate.

Place Black Kt at K4, and Black K at K5. Before
proceeding to cover the squares around the K we will
select the mating men. WP placed at K2 would enable
us to mate by P x Kt at either Black's Q6 or B6. WRs
placed at QB3 and KKt3 would protect the P, and also
enable us to mate by R x Kt at either QB5 or KKt5.
WP at K6 and WQ at K8 would enable us to mate by
Q x Kt at QB3 or KKt3, also by P x Kt at Q2 or KB2.
We accordingly select these men, place them on their
allotted squares, and thus insure a mate after each move
of the Kt. Now we proceed to cover the flight squares—
viz., Q4, KB4, Q5, and KB5. The first two may be
covered by placing a WP at K3. The other two may be

covered by exchanging the P at K6 for a WB. We now find that the square the Kt stands on must be covered. It cannot be covered with a WP, as it would prevent either of the Rs from mating; a WB placed at QKt8 or KR8 would answer, but placing a piece on the board for no other purpose than to cover one square would be a waste of material. It must be remembered that economy of force is one of the principal features of a problem. Bearing this in mind, and considering that we have yet to place the WK on the board, we look to see if it would be of utility, as it is essential for such an important piece to be of use. We find that the three squares, Q5, K5, and KB5, which the two Bs are employed to cover, could be covered equally as well by placing WK at K6. Standing at K6 the K can capture Kt at Q2 or KB2, and give dis. mate in the same way as we did with the QB. Therefore we place WK as suggested, and remove the Bs from the board. Our next step is to prevent White from having the choice of more than one mating move after the Kt plays. As the position stands White has the choice of 3 and 4 mating moves after each move of Black's. These we will prevent by placing WPs at QB6, KKt6, QB4, and KKt4. The two latter Ps recover Q5 and KB5, and enable it to form a good key by removing WK to K7 :

BLACK.

WHITE.

White to play and mate in 2 moves.

H

This Problem is a very good specimen of the "Waiting-move" class. It will be seen that after the key-move (K to K6) is made, White cannot mate until Black plays.

Black Pawns play an active part in chess problems, and are ever useful in warding off checks, stopping and covering squares, hindering dual mates, and preventing unintended solutions. Although a P is prevented from moving backwards, like a piece, and from capturing an opposing man which obstructs its onward march, the restrictions are atoned for by the privilege it has of moving one way and capturing in another, a *modus operandi* which adds considerably in constructing. As in a game a Black P is at its full strength when threatening to become promoted. Its full power may be conceived by placing one at K7, and minor White pieces at Q sq and KB sq. Standing thus the P has choice of three moves and can become Q, R, B, or Kt on each, and so cause upwards of 12 variations. This idea, however, is too elaborate for a two move problem, and can only be partly worked out in a three mover, as we have shown. The play of a Black P can be introduced into a two move problem in a variety of ways. It may be allowed to move to one of the eighth squares, be exchanged for one of the four pieces, and each exchange made to cause White to vary his play. This theme cannot be carried out without a dual mate occurring, owing to the combined power of R and B being invested in the Q. Black P may be placed at K2 and White men at Q6 and KB6, giving the P choice of four moves and making each cause a different mate. Again, a position can be set up with the idea of effecting mate by P x P *en passant*.

As illustrations of how Black Ps may be used in stopping squares around the BK, and at the same time be useful in causing White to vary his play, we give two problems, which are alike in construction, yet having different ideas and solutions.

Problem A.

White—K at KR4, Q at QR3, R at K8, Bs at KKt8, and KR2, Kts at QB sq, and QR7. Total, 7.

Black—K at K5, Ps at Q5, K4, KB2, and KB5. Total, 5.

White to play and mate in two moves.

, Problem B.

White—K at KR4, Q at QR3, R at KB8, B at KKt8, Kts at QB sq, and QR7. Total 6.

Black—K at K5, Ps at Q5, K4, KB2, and KB5. Total, 5.

White to play and mate in two moves.

Problem A is solved by 1 Q to R6, allowing BK the choice of four squares to play on, and giving five different mates, one of the principal being caused by P to B6.

Problem B is solved by 1 R x P. It contains three variations, the idea being the ingenious mate by discovery which is given when Black plays K to Q4.

CASTLING.—Should castling be allowed in problems? We distinctly answer "No." Castling should be avoided on White's side as well as Black's, except in cases where it can be proved that K and R, or R's had not previously moved.

Some composers contend that, when K and R stand on their original squares with no piece between, and no square attacked which the K has to pass over, it is fair to assume that neither K or R had previously moved, and that castling may be done. Others contend that there should be no presumption in favour of White, but there may be in favour of Black. We contend that there should be no presumptions on either side. If it is fair to assume that White or Black may castle with K and R, it is equally fair to assume that K may castle without a R. Remembering that "when the odds of either Rook or both Rooks are given, the player giving the odds shall be allowed to move his King as in castling, and as though the Rooks were on the board," it follows that if assumptions are admissible, any problem having a K on its original square, no piece on the same rank and no square attacked which the K has to pass over would in all probability be unsound, as K could leap to KKt sq or QB sq.

Here, for instance, we have a problem apparently sound—

White—K at K6, Q at K2, Kt at KKt4. Total, 3.

Black—K at K sq, B at KR3, Ps at KR2, and K6. Total, 4.

White proceeds with 1 Q to QKt2, Black may reply with 1 K to Q sq or K to KB sq, then mate follows by 2 Q to QKt8 or Q to KR8 acc. If castling were admissible, the problem would be unsolvable in two moves, as Black could play K to QB sq or K to KKt sq. We will now place a Black R at KR sq and have a position in which it would appear that Black would be justified in castling with KR. It will be seen that there is a mate provided for such a move. Those who contend that an assumption should be allowed would, without hesitation, say that the problem is sound, as mate can be effected in all cases even if Black castles with KR. We say that if it is fair to assume that Black had not previously moved K and KR, it would be also fair to assume that Black gave the odds of QR, and that he would be as much justified in castling on Q's side ; therefore, if he castles on Q's side, there is no mate, as before, and the problem is unsound.

The following problem, taken from " Letts' Household Magazine " Problem Tourney, is another instance of the ill-effects of an assumption :—

White—K at K sq, Q at Q4, Rs at KR sq, and QR8, B at KKt5, Ps at KR5, and KR6. Total, 7.

Black—K at KB sq, Rs at K sq, and KKt sq, B at K4, P at Q3. Total, 5.

White to play and mate in two moves.

The problem can be solved by 1 Q x B. The conductor of the tourney being " strongly of opinion that where WK and R are placed as they are the solver has a right to assume that they have not been moved, and that he can therefore castle," the solver accordingly cooked the problem by castling. In reference to the dictum laid down by the tourney conductor, " Land and Water " says :—" We feel called upon to take issue directly and unhesitatingly. The true principle is that nothing whatever should be presumed in favour of White. This is, indeed, now a settled rule, and in obedience to that rule we were compelled not long since to reject a very pretty two-mover, sent to us by Fritz Peipers, of San Francisco. The first move in that composition was P x P *en passant*, and if that move could be made, there was a solution in two moves, as intended; but we should have had to assume that Black, on his last move, had pushed a Pawn two squares. That, as being an assumption in favour of White, could not, as we considered, be entertained. If any presumption is to be made at all, it should be in favour of Black."

The chess column of "Land and Water," which was under the able editorship of Mr W. N. Potter, took a right stand in tabooing any supposition, assumption, or presumption on White's part, but was wrong, as we have shown, in admitting such on Black's part. If assumption were allowed, White in many cases could not mate. We have seen a very pretty prize problem in which a WP stood at K5 and a Black P at Q4. The solution commenced with the move of a Q, the problem was sound, but would not be so if assumption were admitted, as White could also proceed by moving KP to Q6 and removing Black's QP from the board.

A chess problem must be a position which could occur in actual play, or, in other words, it must be one that can be arrived at by a series of legal moves. It does not matter how improbable such a series of moves may be; if they are possible, the position is possible. If one cannot be reached by a series of legal moves, it is impossible, consequently unsound, and not fit for publication. Mostly all problems are improbable positions, hence the moves of a game played up to one would also be improbable. Take, for instance, the first prize three-mover in the Irish Chess Association Problem Tourney. In it we have a Black K opposed to five White pieces, one of which is a Q. Such a position, although in every way meritorious, is highly improbable, yet it can be arrived at by a series of legal moves.

When playing a game once, Mr J. H. Blackburne saw a mate about twelve moves ahead, he sacrificed each of his pieces in such a way as to cause his opponent to hem in his own K, and so enabled the champion to give smothered mate. The position, K and Kt against the full forces of the opposite side, was improbable, nevertheless, it is an instance of such having occurred in actual play.

When K and R or Rs stand on their original squares in a problem with no other piece on the same rank, it would be impossible to prove that neither had not previously moved. On the other hand, in some cases, it is possible to prove, as we will show, that they had moved.

Here we have a position with the two Ks and four Rs standing on their original squares :—

BLACK.

WHITE.

White to play and mate in 2 moves.

White commences with 1 Q to K5, and mates next move even if Black castles on either side. We will show, however, that neither White nor Black can castle.

It is immaterial to the problem whether White is able to castle or not; nevertheless, as illustration, we will demonstrate that he had moved each of his R's, and therefore cannot castle. We will also prove that Black had previously moved his K, and consequently cannot castle.

Black captured two pieces, one is White's KB taken

at KB sq, the other is the QB. White captured seven pieces. There are only five Black pieces off the board, therefore it follows that Black must have promoted two P's—viz., KKtP and QRP. The former took QB on KR's file and became a piece at KR8. The latter, not having made a capture, passed on to QR8, where it was promoted. To allow of the promotions White must have moved each of his Rs, and therefore cannot now castle.

White's QP, at K4, took one piece, his QBP, at Q3, took one, and his QKtP, at QB6, took one. His QRP must have been promoted to a KB. This accounts for the KB standing at R4. To become a KB the RP must have reached a White square on the last rank, the only White square it could have reached is QB's 8th, and to reach it it must have captured four pieces; in doing so it must have given ch at Q7, causing Black's K to move, therefore Black cannot now castle.

On showing the position to several expert solvers, they at once made the key-move, and, for Black's defence, proceeded to castle. None of them were convinced that Black could not castle until it was demonstrated to them. They then admitted the accuracy of the problem.

ANCIENT PROBLEMS.—In taking notes of the progress and improvements of the problem art through successive ages and different countries, no one could avoid being wonderfully surprised at its manifold transformations and the curious contrast which presents itself on comparing the problems of different ages together. Our ancestors would appear to have been very well satisfied in carrying out their ideas, regardless of any rigid rules or regulations.

When problems were first composed there were no set rules or chess laws, and, as many of us know, the moves of most of the pieces were altogether different to those of the present day. The original movement of the King or " Rey," as it was first called in Europe, appears to have been very limited, since he was restricted from moving at all, except by the necessity of extricating him-self from an adverse check. About the beginning of the thirteenth century he had the power of playing one square directly, but was not permitted to move or capture.

diagonally. He also had a peculiar privilege, derived from the Oriental game, which allowed him to move and make a capture similar to the Knight, on his first move, provided he had not been checked. The Queen could make a move of only one square at a time, and that on a diagonal; but a Queen promoted from a Pawn was allowed to make a move of two squares diagonally. The Bishop, up to the time of the introduction of chess into England in the 13th century was termed Alfyn, and had no power over any square except the third from which it stood, on its own diagonal line, he was not permitted to move to a greater or less number. To compensate for this limited action he was allowed to vault over any piece in his way to get to the third square from him. Castling was altogether unknown in India, it being an innovation of comparatively recent date, and supposed to have been originated in Italy. The Rook, otherwise had the same power as it has now, and was consequently the most powerful piece on the board. The moves of the Knight also remained unchanged. This ancient mode of moving the pieces was in vogue up to the year 1500. As an illustration of one composed according to the old rules, we give what is believed to be the oldest problem on record. It is to be found in an ancient Persian M.S. which is preserved in a museum in London, and is attributed to Caliph Kalifen Mutasim Billah, who reigned in Bagdad 833 to 842.

THE OLDEST PROBLEM.

White—K at Q sq, Q at Q5, Rs at QR7, and QB7, Bs at QB sq, and KB5, Kts at QKt6, and Q4, Ps at QKt2, and K2. Total, 10.

Black—K at Q Kt sq, Q at QKt8, Rs at KKt3, and KR5, Bs at QR3, and KKt5, Kts at QKt2, and QB4, Ps at QR4, QR5, Q3, and K4. Total, 12.

White to play and mate in nine moves.

Solution : 1 R at R7 x Kt ch, 1 Kt x R (B cannot take R as it commands only the 3rd square), 2 R to B8 ch (B could take R here, but if it did so mate would follow in four moves), 2 K to R2, 3 Kt to Kt5 ch, 3 K x Kt at Kt6, 4 R to B6 ch, 4 K x Kt (K would be *en prise* to Q on any diagonal square next her only), 5 B to Q7 ch (having the power of checking across another piece), 5 K to Kt5, 6 R to Kt6 ch, 6 K to B 4, 7 R to Kt5 ch, 7 K to Q5, 8 P to K3 ch, 8 K to Q6, 9 B to KB5 mate (were it not for the perpetual ch BK could leap like a Kt, and so escape).

This problem, like all others for many centuries after its time, is more of an end game, in which Black's moves are forced.

About the year 1300 it would appear as if economy of force, neatness of construction, and an avoidance of perpetual check was more observed. As an illustration we give one

COMPOSED IN 1300.

White—R at Q6, Ps at QB4, and K2.

Black—K at K4.

White to play and mate in three moves.

This problem, it will be noticed, is minus the WK, a piece which was not placed on the board except when made use of. The solution commences with 1 R to KB6, then, as BK could not move or capture diagonally, he must play to K5, 2 R to B5, 2 K to K6 or Q5, 3 R to K5 or B4 accordingly, giving mate.

The simple idea of mating K with R at the side of the board appears to have received considerable attention from our ancestors. This, however, is not to be wondered at, considering that the R was the most powerful piece. It would also appear as if they did not refrain from working on each other's ideas, as the following problems will show. In each the K moves as he does now-a-days, a fact which shows about what time our rules came into existence.

COMPOSED IN 1320.

White—K at K6, Rs at Q6, and KB6.

Black—K at K sq.

White to play and mate in two moves.

This problem was the harbinger of two-movers. Like many others of its time, it admits of a second solution. It will be seen that either R may play to the file next it, and so force Black K to play, and allow of mate on next move.

The same idea converted into a three-mover appeared as follows :—

COMPOSED IN 1350.

White—K at K5, Rs at Q5, and KB5.

Black—K at K2.

White to play and mate in three moves.

The author's solution is given as 1 R to Q sq, 2 K to Q6, 3 R to B8 mate, but either R may play to any square of the file on which it stands excepting the 7th and 8th, thus the problem produces ten key-moves.

The same position, moved one square down, appeared in the year 1400 as a four-mover, after which it was given as a five-mover, then as a six-mover, and finally as a seven-mover, the position being moved down one square on each occasion by different composers.

Problems with the ancient method of moving the pieces ceased to be composed about the middle of the 16th century, Damiano, Lucena, and Guarinus being the last of the race. In the 17th century the art took the form of middle games, Greco, Palerio, Salvio, Gianutio, and Augustus Selenus, the Duke of Brunswick, being the principal composers of that time. In the 18th century Stamma and Lolli came to the fore and pleased the problem world with a series of positions ranging from three moves up, the most of which commence with a check, which is kept up to the final move.

Compositions of the time of Stamma, Lolli and Ponziani —over a century ago—commence with a murderous ch, which is kept up to the final move, leaving Black only one forced line of play, and abound in dual continuations, dual and triple mates, and invariably admit of a profusion of key-moves, which were seemingly ignored when not interfering with the theme. As time wore on rules were gradually recognised, variations introduced, superfluous pieces left the board, ideas became more defined, and thus we passed from the grub to the butterfly, from the bud to the full blown rose. It was not until Staunton's time, however, that any visible improvement appeared. Many fine compositions came to light then, one of the most notable being the famous Indian problem, which we believe to be the first composed on the now well worn principle of masking the power of White's forces. Like many other problems of bygone days it admits of several key-moves.

THE INDIAN PROBLEM.

White—K at QR sq, R at Q sq, Bs at KR6, and KKt2, Ps at KKt4, KB2, QKt3, and QR2. Total, 8.

Black—K at K5, Kt at KB6, Ps at K4, QKt3, and QKt4. Total, 5.

White to play and mate in four moves.

White may proceed with any waiting move, of which he has the choice, then 2 B to B sq, 3 R to Q2, and 4 R to Q4 double ch and mate. The author's intended key is 1 B to B sq.

The following is a rendering of the Indian theme by J. Rayner:—

White—K at KB7, B at QR3, Kts at Q2, and KB3, Ps at QR4, and QKt5. Total, 6.

Black—K at Q4, P at QKt2. Total, 2.

White to play and mate in three moves.

Solution: 1 B to B8, 2 K to K7, 3 K to K6 dis. mate.

We will now borrow our ancestors idea of mating with the Rook and construct a three-move problem accordingly. Selecting a central sq for Black's K, we place him at K4, form a barricade of his third rank by placing WK at K7; now place WR at QR4, and the BK will be left with the choice of two squares to play to. As our object is to give mate with the R we must, after the K moves, prevent him from returning to K4 sq, and from moving further. If BK plays to Q4, White could play a Kt to Q3 and so prevent him from returning, and from going on to QB4, his QB3 may be covered by placing a WP at QKt5. Now to allow of a second move for Black, place a BP at say KB3, and in order to mate by

R to Q4 place a WP at K3. Our next step is to remove
the Kt and try the effects of 1 BK to KB4. Here it will
be seen that WKt to KB3 would cover two of the flight-
squares, and a WP at KR5 would cover the third. It
follows that the Kt must stand at K sq in order to play
to either Q3 or KB3, and another BP must be placed on
the board to allow of Black's second move in the second
variation. Therefore place a BP at Q3 and WKt at K sq.
We now try the effects of P to Q3, and find that it
in no way prevents mate, as White can play Kt to B3 ch,
then K must move, and R can mate; likewise if P to
B4, Kt plays to Q3 ch, and mate follows on next move.
As a key move, Kt from B2 to K sq would do, so placing
Kt at QB2 completes our problem, which is as follows :—

White—K at K7, R at QR4, Kt at QB2, Ps at QKt5,
K3, and KR5. Total, 6.

Black—K at K4, Ps at Q3, and KB3. Total, 3.

White to play and mate in three moves.

Kohtz and Kockelkorn have said that to make a
pleasing problem its mating position must, in a certain
degree, be very elegant.   A feeble key leaves less discon-
tent behind when a pretty ending follows; but a feeble
ending weakens the impression even of the prettiest
beginning. This truth is, unfortunately, too often overlooked, and the consequence is that many fine ideas
having good key-moves, lamentably break down in the
mates, and make no favourable impression on the solver's
mind.   It is necessary, therefore, to build up pretty
mating positions. The squares around the BK should
be clean, i.e., not doubly guarded—there should be no idle
spectators on the board. Several inactive White pieces,
which were used in the beginning, or to take part in
some other variation, spoil the effect of the problem.
In two-movers of many variations, idle pieces are un-
avoidable in some of the mates, but in problems from
three moves up they are inexcusable. In the highest
order of problems all the White men on the board are
used in each mate, and some of the squares around the K
are blocked by Black men, which take active part in
other variations.

We will now set up a position, in which three men are to take part in giving mate, and compose a problem accordingly. Place White Q at Q4, B at Q2, and P at Q5. Black—K at Q3 and P at QB2. Now play B to QKt4 ch. If Black replies with P to B4 our intention is to play P x P *en pass*, and so give double ch and mate. We make these moves, and find that the WP must be protected and two squares guarded. WR placed at QB8 and a Black Kt at K3 answers our purpose, and we have a mating position in which Q, B, and P combined give mate. Now retract the moves. As it is a three move problem we are constructing, we must allow Black to make a move prior to playing B to Kt4, therefore place K at K2. Standing thus Black has choice of three moves for K and seven for Kt, one of which is Kt x Q. We must now proceed to arrange a mate in reply to Kt x Q. Place a WB at KR3, WKt at KR6, and a Black P at KB3, and our position is as follows :

White—Q at Q4, R at QB8, Bs at Q2, and KR3, Kt at KR6, P at Q5.

Black—K at K2, Kt at K3, Ps at QB2, and KB3.

Now if 1 Kt x Q, then 2 B to Kt4 ch, &c. If instead of taking Q Black played Kt to Q sq, we could proceed by Q to B5 ch, driving the K to Q sq, and in order to mate place a WP at KKt7, and play Q to KB8 mate. To prevent the P from causing a dual solution place a BKt at KKt sq. Our next step is to try each of Black's moves. If 1 K to Q2, 2 KB x Kt ch, and Kt mates on next move. If 1 K to Q3, 2 B to Kt4 ch, 2 P to QB4, 3 P x P *en pass* double ch and mate ; if 2 Kt to B4, 3 B x Kt mate ; and if 2 K to Q2, 3 KB x Kt mate. 1 P to KB4, 2 Q to K5, &c., 1 other, 2 P x Kt, &c. In this problem we were unable to make use of the WK ; it must, however, be placed on the board—Q sq would do. Next form a key and our problem would be completed. Kt from KKt4 to R6 would do for key.

Final position—

White—K at Q sq, Q at KKt sq, R at QB sq, Bs at Q2, and KR3, Kt at KR6, Ps at Q5, and KKt7. Total, 8.

Black—K at K2, Kts at K3, and KKt sq, Ps at QB2, and KB3.   Total, 5.

White to play and mate in three moves.

This problem, constructed as we write, as most of the others are, may contain a second solution, if so the key could be altered or a Black P added as required.   Being of the attacking class it will admit of additional Black forces.

Our previously constructed three-mover was worked out with a set idea; the present one, as seen, is worked out by first setting up a mating position and then putting back the moves.

It will be seen that White can effect mate on his second move after several replies of Black's.   This is allowable, and does not seriously detract from the merits of a problem.   At the same time it must be remembered that the best constructed and highest order of problems are those in which the mate cannot be effected in less than the required number of moves.   However, the essential condition of a problem is to move in such a way that Black cannot prolong the game beyond the number of moves given, and if he makes a weak reply it is White's duty to avail himself of it.

HELP-MATE PROBLEMS.—Concerning the Eastern origin of chess, it is curious to notice the influences exerted by contemporary mythology.   Sacred regard for the person of a king invested that piece with immunity from actual capture, and entitled him to warning of every intended assault.   So, also, implicit belief in happiness after death induced a desire for death, and suggested "The losing Game," "Suicidal Problems," and another class of problems not hitherto much noticed, in which *both players cncur* in endeavouring to effect the speediest mate—the one receiving and the other giving it—and which we term Help-mate problems.   This class so far differs from the others that Black, instead of resisting, assists in every possible way in aiding White to mate him.   Though frequently introduced they have not been favourably received, owing, probably, to their simplicity of construction and want of variations.   Nevertheless, they can illustrate how easily an open non-mating position may be transformed into a mate of beauty and elegance. The only difficulty in composing them is to prevent neither side from having more than one line of play. They are composed principally on the inductive plan. An ingenious or pleasing mate is set up, after which the men are removed to different squares, the re-placing of which forms the solution.

For instance, form a mating position by placing WK at KKt4, and Kts at QB2, and KB6. Black—K at K5, R at Q6, and P at K4. Remove Kt at B6 to K8, P to K2, WK to R4, R to KKt6, Kt to K sq, and the problem is as follows :—

White—K at KR4, Kts at K sq, and K8. Total, 3.

Black—K at K5, R at KKt6, P at K2. Total, 3.

White, with Black's help, to mate in three moves.

The following are fair specimens of the help-mate class :—

An old Indian problem unearthed from a forgotten source.

White—K at KKt sq, R at KR8, B at KKt3, Kt at KR5, Ps at KR2, KB6, K7, Q6, QB5, and QR5. Total, 10.

Black—K at QR sq, B at QB sq, Ps at QR3, KKt7, and KR6. Total, 5.

White to play, and his King, instead of giving, receives mate through the treachery of his own forces in three moves.

Solution : 1 B to B2, 1 K to R2, 2 Kt to Kt3, 2 B to Kt2, 3 Kt to R sq, 3 P x Kt (Q) mate.

By Mr. W. A. Shinkman, Grand Rapids, Mich., U.S.A.

White—K at KKt5, R at KB sq, B at KKt sq. Total, 3.

Black—K at KR8, Rs at K8, and QR5, B at KR7, Kt at K7, Ps at KKt2, 5, and 7, KB4, and 6. Total, 10.

Black to play and move in such a manner as to allow White to mate in three moves.

Solution : 1 B to K4 or Q3, 1 B to B2 dis. ch, 2 K to R7, 2 K to R4, 3 Kt to B5, 3 B to Kt3 mate.

Adapted by Mr. Porterfield Rynd from a problem by Mr. T. B. Rowland.

White—K at QR8, B at KB sq, Kts at K5, and K7. Total, 4.

Black—K at K5, Ps at Q4, and KB4. Total, 3.

White, with Black's help, to mate in three moves.

Solution : 1 Kt (K5) to B6, 1 P to Q5, 2 Kt to Q5, 2 P to Q6, 3 B mates.

On introducing the latter, Mr. Rynd recounts the circumstances attending his discovery of Help-mates. It is to the effect that when playing a game in which two Kts and two Ps were opposed to his B and P, and having heard that the two Kts could not win, he.manœuvred so warily that he got an opportunity of sacrificing his B and P for his opponent's two Ps, and thus escaped with a draw. Not long after he observed the following position in a game played by others :—

White—K at KR sq, Kts at KKt5, and KKt7.

Black—K at KKt5.

Black had just taken a White Pawn, reducing White's forces to two Kts and it was White's turn to move. "I saw it was a draw," says Mr. Rynd, "and was on the point of offending against bystander's etiquette by so exclaiming, when I remembered I shouldn't. My silence on that occasion gave me the idea of Help-mates. Plainly White could not mate unless Black accommodated him, and even then I did not think it possible. However, as the game was actually played, White mated in three moves ! So far for narration. Now for explanatory remarks—I classify play and problems into three classes—ordinary, suicidal or losing, and helping or colluding. In ordinary play and problems the players contend, each trying to avoid mate of himself and to effect mate of his adversary. In what are called (but not without inaccuracy) suicidal problems, and also in playing the "losing game," the players still contend, though for a different object, each then trying to avoid mate of his adversary and to effect mate of himself. In

Help-mate problems, and also in Help-mate games (such as the Fool's Mate, and other short games of the kind) contention is at an end, and each player does his best to aid in effecting the desired mate, whether it be of himself or of his adversary. In Help-mate Problems particularly, this new element of co-operation is productive of much pleasing and instructive variety."

CONDITIONAL PROBLEMS.—"A spirit of weariness moves amongst problemists, and this whether they be solvers or composers. The old stock dishes are now viewed by them with indifference, if not aversion. They begin to ask why nothing but beef, pork, and mutton should be eaten. It is true, indeed, that their desires have already been partially met. Their caterers have introduced that pheasant amongst problems, the self-mate. This departure from the recognised fare has been condemned by some old stagers, but it was too welcome a change not to be in the main cordially approved of, and it is not deniable that a taste for self-mates is spreading rapidly. To those who have during evil days stood by the self-mate its ever-increasing popularity must be highly gratifying, but why should we stay where we are? There is un-doubtedly room on the chess board for an almost infinite variety for puzzles. The form of one of Mr Planck's problems, published in this column some little time ago, suggested to us the idea that stale mates were worthy of consideration by composers, as likely to be a refreshing change from either direct mates or suicidal mates. Upon examining Mr Rowland's puzzle, published in our issue of October 4, it appeared to us that a problem similar in form, but not specifying which Pawn was to mate, could be manufactured. Such a proposition as "White to play and mate with one of his Pawns" would not have answered with Mr. Rowland's problem, for it will be found that in that composition mate can be given within the prescribed number of moves, as well by the KP as by the KKtP. This fact is sufficient to show what ingenious and delusive puzzles could be framed, and it conjures up pictures of solvers wondering within themselves which of those Pawns is the mating Pawn. An agreeable vista of variety is opened out by East Marden's remarks published hereunder; and the puzzle with which he concludes will doubtless give pleasure to our solvers, especially if it be as new to them as it is to us. Therein two Pawns take part in the mate, one of them having to check at the sixth move, and the other to mate on the seventh move, the solver being left to find out which Pawn has to give the penultimate check and which to give the mate. Problems are conceivable having nothing to do with a mate. A position could be manufactured in which it would be very difficult to discover whether it were a possible or an impossible position. A question of this kind, assuming a well-constructed composition, would yield much interest and pleasure to expert solvers. In another kind of puzzle they might be asked to find out the original file of some particular Pawn. When it is considered that a Pawn on QKt seventh could have been the KKtP, it is obvious that here would be much scope for constructive ingenuity on the part of composers and for analytical research on the part of the solvers. Then again there are the curious results that may issue from promotions. It would be quite possible for two Bishops to be on the board, both of which had changed their colour, the King's Bishop of the White forces assuming a black diagonal, and the Queen's Bishop, not to be outdone, getting on to a White diagonal. This, perhaps, would be more humorous than analytically edifying, but other and more useful effects could be extracted from • the law of promotion. For instance, White may have undertaken to mate with a Bishop, but through incautiously allowing Black to draw a Pawn from its file may find himself left with King and two Bishops of the same colour. Of course under such circumstances, or indeed with any number of unicoloured Bishops, unless there be other forces, he could not give mate. These hints are sufficient to show that there lie hidden in the chess board and waiting their day all manner of subtle and sparkling conceptions."—"Land and Water."

One word as to the benefit derived from problem composition. Does it improve a chess player? We answer emphatically yes. A player by composing will learn the different and manifold combinations of the pieces and

how to accomplish the mate with certain men placed in
certain positions, and will also learn with a keen percep-
tion the full and complete power of every piece, even the
unobtrusive Pawn—which undoubtedly increases his
power of combination as well as insight into the game.
One other word in reference to the comparison between
composers and chess players. We hold that every chess
player may and can compose problems, and, indeed,
become a fair composer, for the whole game is a great
problem, and move by move it is reduced to one of fewer
moves, and he needs but to remodel his ending position
in order to make a problem out of it. Herr Anderssen,
the great chess player of Germany, in his early days
composed a problem which for beauty of idea and construction remains unsurpassed to this day. It does not
so readily follow, however, that every problemist may
become a good chess player. The biographies of composers
prove that they are only mediocre players. There may
be an explanation of this in the fact that they, being
peculiarly gifted in the art of composing problems,
become so infatuated with it that they neglect the game,
and consequently do not attain to any degree of profici-
ency in it. But we imagine that it is more logical to say
that as they have no taste for the game, consequently
they possess no talent, for taste and talent are twin sisters.
And finally, as hundreds and hundreds of problems have
been composed and published, the question might arise,
are there any new ideas on the science of problem composition? We answer the query by saying that all the
fundamental ideas have been discovered, and that the
newness and originality of a problem consist, not in the
discovery of new principles, but in the combination of old
ideas. A new invention consists not in the discovery of
new principles, but in combining those already known,
so as to accomplish different purposes, and on this
patents are granted. One composer arranges his ideas
in one way, another in another, each displaying his
style and originality by the new arrangement of old
ideas, and the greater the facility with which he forms
new combinations the more numerous will be his compositions.

NOTATION.

NOTATION AND ABBREVIATIONS.

THE squares are numbered from one to eight, counting from each side, and are called after the pieces which occupy the first rank at the beginning of a game : K on King sq, Q on Queen sq, KB on KB sq, &c. The following diagram will better illustrate the notation :—

BLACK.

QRsq QR8	QKtsq QKt8	QBsq QB8	Qsq Q8	Ksq K8	KBsq KB8	KKtsq KKt8	KRsq KR8
QR2 QR7	QKt2 QKt7	QB2 QB7	Q2 Q7	K2 K7	KB2 KB7	KKt2 KKt7	KR2 KR7
QR3 QR6	QKt3 QKt6	QB3 QB6	Q3 Q6	K3 K6	KB3 KB6	KKt3 KKt6	KR3 KR6
QR4 QR5	QKt4 QKt5	QB4 QB5	Q4 Q5	K4 K5	KB4 KB5	KKt4 KKt5	KR4 KR5
QR5 QR4	QKt5 QKt4	QB5 QB4	Q5 Q4	K5 K4	KB5 KB4	KKt5 KKt4	KR5 KR4
QR6 QR3	QKt6 QKt3	QB6 QB3	Q6 Q3	K6 K3	KB6 KB3	KKt6 KKt3	KR6 KR3
QR7 QR2	QKt7 QKt2	QB7 QB2	Q7 Q2	K7 K2	KB7 KB2	KKt7 KKt2	KR7 KR2
QR8 QRsq	QKt8 QKtsq	QB8 QBsq	Q8 Qsq	K8 Ksq	KB8 KBsq	KKt8 KKtsq	KR8 KRsq

WHITE.

The abbreviations (in general use) are : K for King, Q for Queen, R for Rook or Castle, B for Bishop, Kt for Knight, P for Pawn, sq for square, ch for check, dis ch for discovered check, dbl ch for double check, en pass for *en passant*, and x for takes.

THE FORSYTH NOTATION.

This is the invention of Mr David Forsyth, a Scottish amateur, and is deserving of attention, as it is the easiest and most concise method for recording positions. It is used chiefly to note positions occurring in actual play, though it is also adopted in several chess columns to save the large amount of space necessary for diagrams. The problem we give on next page can be represented in the Notation as follows :

8 | B 7 | 2 *s* 3 S 1 | 2 *s k* 2 *p* 1 | 1 *p* 4 B 1 | 1 P 3 P 2 | 4 S 2 Q | 7 K.

The divisions represent the eight ranks ; the figures represent the number of vacant squares ; the large capitals, White men ; and the italics, Black men.

Reading the chess board or diagram as one would read a page of a book, beginning at Black Q's R sq, it will be found that the eight squares in the first row are vacant, this is accordingly represented by 8. In the second row there are a WB and seven vacant squares, hence B 7. In the third row there are two vacant squares, a Black Kt, three vacant squares, a White Kt, and one vacant square ; thus 2 *s* 3 S 1 represents it. And so on throughout the remaining rows of squares. It will be noticed that S is given for Kt ; this is to prevent confusion with K for King.

Various improvements were suggested on the system when it was first published in the "Glasgow Weekly Herald," in February 1883 the most important being to ignore the division of the board into rows, and to add together the vacant squares at the end of one row and at beginning of the next. The position we give would thus be represented by—8 B 9 *s* 3 S 3 *s k* 2 *p* 2 *p* 4 B 2 P 3 P 6 S 2 Q 7 K. The position is much more easily set up from the first variety. The modified form can be advantageously used for telegraphic purposes.

By George J. Slater, Bolton.

Awarded First Prize in the "Milwaukee Telegraph" Tourney.

BLACK.

WHITE.

White to play and mate in 2 moves.

During the progress of the game between Steinitz and Zukertort in the first round of the London International Tournament, 1883, a position was telegraphed to the Glasgow Chess Club, and appeared in diagram form in the "Glasgow Herald" of the following morning. The modified form of the notation was used, and the Black pieces were distinguished from the White by their names being misspelt. It rarely happens that chess positions are thought worth the cost of telegraphing, but a code on the following principle is suggested as the briefest adaptation of the system for telegraphic purpose:—Let K, Q, B, S, R, P stand for White King, Queen, Bishop, Knight, Rook, and Pawn respectively, and let the same letters, followed by a vowel, represent the Black pieces. Also let the letters C, D, F, G, H, L, M, N, T, V stand for the figures 1, 2, 3, 4, 5, 6, 7, 8, 9, and

Ó respectively, in accordance with which arrangement Cv represents 10, Ch 15, Dl 26, and so forth. The position in the diagram represented in the modified form of the notation by 8 B 9 *s* 3 S 3 *s k* 2 *p* 2 *p* 4 B 2 P 3 P 6 S 2 Q 7 K, could be reduced to the following telegraphic message :—

Nbtsafsfsakadpadpagbdpfplsdqmk.

These letters could be grouped into a few words.

In chess columns in which diagrams are frequently indistinct it is advisable to represent problems also in the Forsyth Notation. The Black pieces should be represented by small italic letters, and the White by Roman capitals. This system appeared in the " Southern Trade Gazette " (Kentucky), and has been adopted by the " Glasgow Weekly Herald ; " and is probably the most convenient for printer and reader.

The notation will be found most useful in making pencilled memoranda of positions in adjourned games and interesting positions in actual play, and the variety of it to be recommended for this purpose is that first given, the Black pieces being represented by letters underlined, and a perpendicular line being drawn at the end of each row of 8 squares, to assist in again setting up the position on the board.

W. W. Morgan Jun., Printer, 17 Medina Road, Holloway, London.

15